What Others Are Saying

Over three decades as a nonprofit chief executive, few things have been more critical to success than that of a well-functioning and strategically powerful board. Too often, a board of directors has challenges that can only be resolved by doing the hard work of identifying and then solving its weaknesses. Mary Hiland does a masterful job guiding the chief executive to help board members identify telltale symptoms and follow them to the problem's root causes. Having taken this journey together, they are then guided along the path toward resolution. **Love Your Board!** *is for any executive director/CEO who wants to help their board achieve its full potential.*

Ted Hart, ACFRE, CAP® | President and CEO, CAF America

Mary's book on governance should be read by every executive director and every board member. It covers everything from recruitment and on-boarding to resolving conflict—and when it is time to "cut the cord" and let unproductive board members go. A well-running board is the one big difference between effective, successful nonprofits and those that wither and die, sometimes in their prime. This book will help your board become the well-honed machine that drives success for your nonprofit.

Linda Lysakowski, ACFRE | Author and Consultant

Mary Hiland hits it out of the park with **Love Your Board!** *She takes you into real-life board issues with all their messy uniqueness. It's a must-read for any nonprofit executive director and a resource I wish I had when I sat in the corner office.*

Joanne Oppelt | Author, Trainer, Consultant, and Growth Coach

Love your board? Really? Is it possible? It sure is. Just ask Mary Hiland. In this remarkable book, Mary brings her wealth of experience and practical insights to a very real problem that's vexed nearly every executive director: how to work with your board. Even if you're not an ED, you're sure to learn from her real-life stories and actionable advice based on her twenty-plus years of coaching and consulting with nonprofits.

Matt Hugg | President and Founder, Nonprofit.Courses

I have known Mary Hiland for almost thirty years. Her experience as an executive director and as a consultant brings to light the real-life challenges of nonprofit executives. She has done the research, walked the path, trained hundreds of nonprofits in better governance, and highlights actionable steps toward maximizing your board's potential. **Love Your Board!** *provides a wealth of invaluable knowledge.*

Patricia Gardner | Former CEO, Silicon Valley Council of Nonprofits | PAG Leadership Consulting

I love this book! It is easy to follow, warm, and congenial. It is evidence-based, and the examples illustrate and move the reader through the processes Mary recommends. The tree metaphor made the book feel like the advice and information given is organic and could become part of the fabric of an organization. I highly recommend it to all executive directors.

Maria Nicolacoudis | CEO, Hearts & Minds Activity Center

Reading this wonderfully supportive, practical, and reflective book will give you the tools you need to help your board overcome its deficiencies and unlock its potential to lead your nonprofit organization brilliantly. **Love Your Board!** *is a must-read for all nonprofit executives, no matter how long in your leadership role.*

Christine Duncan | CEO, YWCA Monterey County

The most common challenge I hear from both first-time and long-term executive directors is how to engage their board to do, well, MORE! If you've had this same thought, Mary Hiland is the perfect person to guide you through the step-by-step, comprehensive journey you can and should take. Mary's vast and extensive experience jumps off every page of this book. I'll encourage every one of my clients to read **Love Your Board!** *so they can glean such valuable information from an industry legend like Mary Hiland!*

Sherry Quam Taylor | CEO of QuamTaylor LLC

I'm a former executive director, and reading **Love Your Board!** *changed my perceptions about boards. Mary gives a well-researched and clearly written view of the role of the board in nonprofit organizations. The Capacity/Connection/Culture framework made complex ideas easy to understand. Applying the framework, sharing real-life stories to illustrate it, and giving practical strategies for working through a myriad of board challenges make this book required reading for executive directors.*

Dee Wischmann, Executive Coach | Former President & CEO, Catholic Charities Silicon Valley

The governing board for a nonprofit organization can make or break an organization's success. Mary writes from her deep experience in the nonprofit sector. She focuses on helping the executive director get to the root causes of a board's failure to reach its potential and then giving the executive director the techniques to help the board overcome whatever is holding it back. I especially appreciated Mary's identification of the three critical factors for successful board development: the use by the executive director of the "nudge" to take the board to the next level, the need for intentionality, and the focus on the indispensable role of the board's chair. I recommend Mary's book for all nonprofit leaders and board members.

Dr. Rob Harter | Executive Director, Christian Center of Park City | Founder and Host of "The Nonprofit Leadership Podcast"

Mary's book is an incredible resource for executive directors. By breaking board improvement into either capacity, connections, or culture and providing case studies, Mary provides clear, actionable steps for proactively responding to any need an executive director might face in working with their board. This is a book to read once and then go back to regularly as different situations arise.

Shawn Gerth | Executive Director, Educare California at Silicon Valley

When plenty of books on nonprofit boards seem to be every bit as complex as their subject, Mary Hiland shows her mastery by taking the opposite approach: she uses simple stories and explanations to help us understand the root causes of nonprofit board dysfunctions and what executive directors can do to help their boards overcome them. I enthusiastically recommend **Love Your Board!** *to my chief-executive peers who want to help their boards thrive.*

Shake Sulikyan | President & Executive Director, ValleyCare Charitable Foundation

It is not productive to be right. It is productive to be clear. Unfortunately in this sector, we have gotten trapped into a 'must do' menu for boards and executive directors rather than collaboratively working our way toward building trusting relationships, healthy culture, and intentional processes that enable our organizations to focus on achieving their intended purpose. This book is a stand-in for executive directors who can't have Mary working with them as a coach.

Gayle L. Gifford, ACFRE | President, Cause & Effect, Inc. | Author and Consultant

LOVE YOUR BOARD!

THE EXECUTIVE DIRECTORS' GUIDE TO DISCOVERING THE SOURCES OF NONPROFIT BOARD TROUBLES AND WHAT TO DO ABOUT THEM

LOVE YOUR BOARD!

THE EXECUTIVE DIRECTORS' GUIDE
TO DISCOVERING THE SOURCES OF
NONPROFIT BOARD TROUBLES AND
WHAT TO DO ABOUT THEM

MARY HILAND, PHD

Love Your Board!: The Executive Directors' Guide to Discovering the Sources of Nonprofit Board Troubles and What to Do about Them

By Mary Hiland, PhD

Editing, book design, and book layout:

Stephen C. Nill, JD, Author Brick Road, a Division of CharityChannel LLC

Published by Mary Hiland | Morgan Hill, California, USA

Copyright © 2021 Mary Hiland

ISBN: 978-1-7371827-0-2

Library of Congress Control Number: 2021909553

13 12 11 10 9 8 7 6 5 4 3 2 1

A Project of

Author Brick Road

Author Brick Road, a division of CharityChannel, leverages its deep publishing experience to empower visionary and transformative leaders to write and publish books of extraordinary impact, clarity, and usefulness.

About the Author

Mary Hiland, PhD is a nonprofit board and leadership development consultant dedicated to assisting nonprofit executives and board members in unleashing their organizational and community impact potential. She works with nonprofit leaders to strengthen the executive/board partnership and develop the board as a powerful force for organizational and mission results. Mary is a coach and mentor for boards, individual board leaders, and executive directors.

Mary has over forty years of experience in the nonprofit sector—twenty-six as an executive. Her executive experience began with a small nonprofit ($100,000 budget), which she grew by leading two nonprofit mergers into one of the largest nonprofits in the California Bay Area—with 530 staff and a budget of $25 million.

Mary has been consulting since 2002, working with several hundred nonprofits, including associations and all-volunteer nonprofits. The focus of her consulting is board development and executive leadership. As a certified Strategic Restructuring Consultant, Mary has trained and consulted with over ninety nonprofits on mergers and strategic alliances, coaching and facilitating nonprofit leaders through all phases of the process.

Mary understands a board's perspective first-hand, having chaired and served for eighteen years on several nonprofit boards.

Mary is a speaker, published author, and researcher. She has presented at numerous conferences, conducts workshops, and is a business professor at DeAnza Community College. She is a contributing author to four books on nonprofit leadership and governance, including *You and Your Nonprofit Board* (2013) and *Leading and Managing in the Social Sector: Introduction and Overview* (2017).

Mary has received numerous awards, including the Silicon Valley Excellence in Nonprofit Leadership Award, Tribute to Women in Industry Achievement Award, Woman of Achievement in Community Service, and the NSFRE Spirit of Philanthropy Award.

Mary obtained her PhD designation in 2006, focusing on nonprofit leadership and governance, doing research on the board chair/executive relationship and effective boards. Mary has three master's degrees: social work, public administration, and organizational development.

Mary is the founder and host of the podcast *Inspired Nonprofit Leadership*.

Learn more about Mary by visiting her website: https://www.hilandconsulting.org/meet-mary/more-about-mary

LinkedIn: https://www.linkedin.com/in/maryhiland

Inspired Nonprofit Leadership Facebook Group: https://tinyurl.com/inspirednonprofitleadership

Company Facebook: https://www.facebook.com/hilandconsulting

Dedication

To my husband Bill and my daughter Elisa for their extraordinary gifts of unconditional love and support.

To nonprofit executives who envision a better future for others and devote themselves to creating it.

Acknowledgments

Joanne Oppelt, consultant and growth coach, for multiple insightful and professional reviews of this book. Reading it through the eyes of her executive director experience was invaluable as was her straight-forward feedback—making it better every time.

Patricia Gardner, PAG Leadership Consulting and former Executive Director of the Silicon Valley Council of Nonprofits, for her careful review of the draft and her eye for diversity, equity, and inclusion. Her suggestions enabled me to better express my personal commitment to those practices and principles and offer practical ways to truly live them in the board room.

Maria Nicolacoudis, Executive Director of Hearts and Minds Activity Center, and Shake Sulikyan, President and Executive Director of ValleyCare Charitable Foundation, who took time out of their extremely busy schedules to thoughtfully review the manuscript. Their feedback, with more than twenty-nine years together as nonprofit executive directors, was both invaluable and encouraging.

Deborah Pruitt, PhD, author, consultant, mentor, and friend. Deborah's review of the culture chapter was critical to helping me tackle such a complex topic in a meaningful yet practical way.

Theresa Kiernan, former executive director, friend, and accountability "buddy" for being my cheerleader. Her review of the book gave me new ideas and a fresh look at material I had immersed myself in for months.

Dee Wischmann, former CEO of Catholic Charities Silicon Valley, who has been my coach for twenty-three years. Every weekly conversation we've had over those many years has contributed beyond measure to my effectiveness, confidence, and success as a nonprofit executive, consultant, and author. Her response to the book and the process has challenged and supported me.

I acknowledge and thank Stephen Nill, CEO of Author Brick Road, my editor, writing coach, longtime colleague, and friend for his wisdom and extensive knowledge of every detail of the process of bringing this book into your hands.

Finally, thank you to all those who have supported and taught me over these many years. What I share here has been enriched by many others' gifts to me of their knowledge, wisdom, and experience.

Contents

Foreword

When I finished reading *Love Your Board!*, the first thing I did was make an extensive list of all of the nonprofit executives that need to read it. It is an essential handbook that executives should keep within arm's reach. I guarantee that during their tenure, they will encounter many—probably all—of the challenges Mary discusses. She shares the wisdom of decades of experience and thorough research in an extraordinarily sensible and accessible book.

There is a brilliance to the simplicity with which Mary composes this book as she focuses on three concepts: capacity, connection, and culture. She analyzes each through two dimensions: people and process. This formula is very clever because it takes advantage of how we best remember things and then consistently applies the two fundamental components of every successful board: people and process. This is a gift to readers who might be surprised at how much they recall after first reading the book.

Even the title, *Love Your Board!*, evoked in me an immediate reaction after I finished my first reading the book: that's it in a nutshell. I haven't heard or read that phrase anywhere else. As a book for chief executives, this is the key to unlocking possibilities.

Making the choice to love something is an act of crossing a threshold into a space of possibilities. This adjustment in thinking is critical and fundamental to success. Though subtle, it is a powerful concept.

When you love your board, you do things differently, your patience and empathy expand, and you become more thoughtful. One of the many things that stand out is how artfully Mary leads us down a path of common-sense thinking. She helps us see the symptoms with great clarity and shows us how to address them and set the board on a productive course. I am confident she accomplishes her goal of saving executives time and resources and lives up to her promise, "You'll have a new understanding, empowering you to uncover the *real* reason you're challenged with the board and identify barriers getting in the way of changing it."

Having spent decades working in the sector, I have personally experienced the frustrations of working with underperforming boards; and it remains prevalent among so many nonprofits today. But executives have a choice to either get lost in the muddle of frustration or make the conscious choice to shift from focusing on the problems to looking for solutions. Mary guides us from identifying the symptoms to applying the best practice.

I love the pragmatic approach—and the clarity with which she presents sound advice. Mary starts with capacity. And as she reminds us throughout the book, it begins with people. In chapter two, she sidesteps the trap of seeking board candidates through the lens of business acumen rather than governing competence. Going right to the heart of it, she asks: do prospective board members have the skills, knowledge, diverse cultural perspectives, and abilities to lead? And as she points out, it's not just board-member composition; it also requires a competent CEO.

On the process side of capacity, she frames it as structure, practices, and policies, emphasizing the critical significance of board meeting preparation and management, as well as the effective use of committees, both of which she traces back to the critical importance of an effective recruitment and onboarding process.

In chapters four and five, Mary takes us to the source of so many difficulties: connections. It's all about relationships, she writes—the quality and the scope. It's interesting that this discussion is at the center of the book because it is at the heart of a well-functioning board. As she explains, having the right people on your board hardly matters if you don't have trusting relationships with them.

Mary tackles what I have seen as the most challenging situation for executive directors: their relationship with the board chair. Mary paints a detailed picture of the range of challenges faced by executive directors. This chapter alone is a valuable primer for any nonprofit chief executive—*especially* those new to the job.

I have painfully observed with many executives I coach the challenges she identifies: micromanagement, being patronized, or experiencing power struggles, to name a few. Mary's honesty and straightforward advice cut right to the essence of the difficulty. As she explains, these behaviors may arise from a lack of understanding of appropriate authority, roles, and boundaries and might be addressed through education. But information alone isn't enough when domineering style and personal needs leave no room for change. This underscores why this book is so important—by being well-informed and deeply knowledgeable about the landscape of nonprofit governance and management, nonprofit executives create a foundation for success.

In the context of the relationship between the chief executive and the board chair, as well as the relationships among board members, Mary elaborates the importance of trust and the levels of trust—the highest being identification-based trust. As she makes clear, trust is personal; you can't trust from an emotionally distant or professional posture. Trust takes openness and communication—and willingness to be vulnerable.

Mary closes *Love Your Board!* with a discussion of culture, which she describes as the deepest dimension of the three. As she writes, it is both complex and expansive and, I have found, the most difficult to get hold of and manage. Though the beliefs that underlie a board's culture are hidden, the behaviors are not; and that is the starting place. "Problems with board culture arise when group beliefs and assumptions get in the way of board effectiveness," she writes. Throughout this chapter, Mary provides many practical examples and approaches to deal with problematic culture, tackling diversity and inclusion along the way. But, as with everything else throughout this highly digestible volume, Mary offers a proven, pragmatic approach that underscores why she is in high demand as an executive coach. I don't want to spoil your own discovery, so I will leave it there.

As she brings things to a close, Mary invites readers to know their personal "why," that passionate connection to the cause that flows from the heart that keeps everyone on mission.

This is a special book steeped in decades of experience and sound research. Each chapter closes with key lessons, and the end of the book is rich with resources. Nonprofit executives who get hold of *Love Your Board!* will surely leave their dog-eared copy on the center of their desk for their successors.

James Mueller

Consultant, James Mueller & Associates LLC
Author, *Onboarding Champions*

Introduction

Do you love your board? Is it producing amazing impact, adding real value, and advancing your mission? Are your board members thought leaders you trust and ask for advice? Is your board your go-to group for support, brainstorming, and resources?

Or do you long for more from your board? What are you hoping for with your board? What's the top-of-mind board problem you want to solve? Are you sure?

Unfortunately, the problems executive directors like you are frustrated with and want fixed are not uncommon. How many times have you experienced or heard from colleagues about board members coming to meetings unprepared? Or they're not engaged and don't participate? Are your board members partners in raising the money your nonprofit needs?

Your board might be micromanaging you, focusing on operations, and confused about the board's role versus staff roles. Do you have a story about your board's recruitment being desperate and needy? Or even nonexistent, relying on you to do it? Do you have a diverse board with an inclusive culture?

While some boards may be great, many fail to develop their full potential for advancing their nonprofit's mission. The potential is real, and when boards are effective, the difference they make is inspiring. I've seen it. I believe in it. I want it for you.

Challenges with boards are frustrating—for you and for many board members. You want to be effective, and problems with your board can get in the way. Board members want to make a real contribution and be effective, too. You're all motivated.

There's lots of information about what exceptional boards are and do. So why aren't more boards being and doing it?

Who Is this Book For?

Are you an executive director or aspiring executive director who yearns to be part of a leadership team that includes a strategically powerful board, only to be frustrated that it can't seem to get past a particular challenge?

Or, maybe your board doesn't have an immediate challenge that you can see; you just know it could do and be more, and you want to take it to the next level—whatever that is.

You may be a new or inexperienced executive director. Or, perhaps you've been in the role for five years or more. You may even be a veteran executive director. This book is for you if you believe in your board's potential and are willing to invest your time and energy to develop it.

It's for you, too, if your board is doing well, but you want to keep it evolving as your nonprofit grows.

No matter what phase of your nonprofit executive career you're in, you can benefit from this book. And so can your board.

To effect change that truly strengthens your board, you need to correctly identify the problem you're trying to fix. The challenge with board development is that the "problem" you think you have, more often than not, is a symptom of something going on at a deeper level. Without identifying and tackling the root cause of a board problem, you won't get real, lasting results. To change or improve your board, you must first answer a critical question. Read on.

A Model for Problems with Boards

As a result of rigorous research, confirmed by years of careful field observation, I learned how board members become effective, engaged thought leaders. I developed an understanding of the causes of problems getting in the way—going deeper than symptoms. Giving you a whole new perspective of your board is what this book is all about. It gives you a new understanding of your board, empowering you to answer the question: *what's the problem, anyway?* You'll learn how to consistently and accurately assess what's really going on and what to do about it.

I reviewed over one hundred cases in which executives or board members requested help with a board challenge. I compared the problem presented with the *real* problem that emerged as we worked together. In many cases, what was *thought* to be the board's issue turned out, on deeper probing, to be something different. I gained key insights into the causes compared to the symptoms.

I discovered all the problems and barriers to board improvement fit within three board dimensions: capacity, connections, and culture. Improving your board's effectiveness—getting it where you want it to be—loving it!—requires understanding and addressing these three dimensions.

Inspired by the giant oak tree in my backyard, I realized boards are like oak trees. Some are majestic and sturdy—giving life through their leaves. Others, though, are scrawny and unhealthy. They need tender loving care to thrive.

Each board is unique. A tree is a perfect metaphor for a nonprofit board and for its three dimensions.

When we look at a tree, our eyes are drawn to the leaves that make up the canopy. The canopy is a metaphor for the many, many things that make up a board's capacity: people, policies, practices, processes, and so on. This is the first dimension.

The branches and trunk represent the many connections between and among you and each board member. Strong relationships and a solid trunk represent the strength and reach of the interpersonal dynamics among board members and with you. This is the second dimension.

The roots of the tree represent board culture—the third dimension. Culture is the often hidden but foundational cause of what happens. Problems rooted in board culture may be the hardest to identify, which is understandable since much of culture is hidden on a day-to-day basis.

The three dimensions of a board—capacity, connections, and culture—involve people and processes. And they're usually interrelated and interdependent. You can't have a healthy tree without leaves, branches, a trunk, and roots. This book is all about helping you have a healthy and robust board—a beautiful, giving asset like a vibrant tree.

How Will You Benefit from This Book?

My goal is to save you time and resources by helping you avoid "barking up the wrong tree." You'll have a new understanding, empowering you to uncover the *real* reason you're challenged with the board and identify barriers getting in the way of changing it.

If you're a new executive, you'll benefit from my tips for preventing common board problems and recognizing the underlying causes for what you're experiencing. Recognizing them is the first step toward having the board of your dreams.

Maybe you've been an executive for several years, and you're not motivated to spend more time than you already are on a board you feel is "just fine." Well, armed with what you'll learn here, I'm confident you won't have to spend more time. And I know you'll discover opportunities to strengthen your board, making your job easier, and getting more impact for your nonprofit.

If you're a long-term executive director with lots of experience working with a board, the model explored here will give you a new perspective. You'll be able to quickly and decisively address early signs and symptoms of issues or, perhaps, simply be inspired to support and appreciate your board in new ways. This book and the resources I provide will serve as a great reference tool for you.

No matter where you are in your career as an executive director, you'll benefit from reading, using, and having this book. You'll learn evidence-based practices and get related resources for developing your board. You'll have, and be able to create on your own, useful tools and strategies for change. You'll know what to do—empowered to act effectively, unleashing the full potential of your board in service to the unique mission of your nonprofit.

How Is This Book Different?

This book is evidence-based. The information and strategies I share with you come from proven practices—my own and others' research—and real experiences of executive directors and board members of what works.

Why I Wrote This Book

I believe nonprofit executive directors are amazing people and can be outstanding leaders. I believe board members really care about the missions of the nonprofits they serve. Both are driven by the desire to make a positive difference.

This book is intended not just to inform you but to *inspire* you to imagine what's possible for your board and have confidence you—and they—can achieve the vision of a board you can and will love.

After over forty years of experience, education, and research in the sector, I've learned a lot. I've seen firsthand, over and over again, what's possible when a board is dynamic, energized, focused, and constructively sharing leadership with the executive. It's what I want for you. I want *that* board to be the norm. Writing this book is a big part of making it happen.

You've been told: *Do this. Do that.* You'll find here a balance between wisdom and experience, inspiration and innovation. Go for it.

What's Coming?

In the coming chapters, we'll explore three categories of information: how boards get better—the success factors you need to know, the three dimensions containing all board problems, and specific tips and strategies for addressing those problems.

In Chapter One, I'll cover how boards "get better." It's only been recently, through research, that we've begun to tease out the critical success factors in board development. You'll learn the three crucial success factors for boards to get better, and three other related factors.

You need to know these before you respond to board problems. I want you to have the success factors in mind as you decide what you'll do to improve your board. These factors apply regardless of the cause of the problem you and your board are working on.

Chapters Two through Six are the core of the book, exploring how problems with your board are manifested in the three dimensions of the model: capacity (like a tree's canopy), connections (its branches and trunk), and culture (the roots). Each dimension is broken down into the people issues and the process issues, and what to do about them.

There are real-life stories as examples throughout the book. Because they are real, the names of the people and organizations have been changed to preserve confidentiality.

After discussing common board problems, you'll get sound practices and action steps for what to do to address problems within each dimension. You can be confident the recommended actions are evidence-based or founded on practices we know work! You also have access to a *Resources Page* by going to https://www.loveyourboardbook.com/resources where I've put lots of tools and information you can use. You'll find references to the *Resources Page* through the book. All of this you can refer to over and over again.

The last chapter, Chapter Seven, pulls it all together. The three dimensions (capacity, connection, culture) are interrelated. I give you helpful examples so that your actions cover all the bases for the board development you need and want.

How to Use This Book

You'll get the most benefit from this book if you read it through. Take a deep dive into capacity, connection, and culture. You'll learn strategies for how to improve your board now and into the future. With new insights, you'll clearly understand your board's functioning and dynamics and what to do to have the best possible team working with you.

Keep the book handy for reference as your board evolves. Especially if you're an experienced executive, you may find your board has all, if not most, of the people and process capacity it needs. You may find the connection and culture chapters most useful—if not now, in the future.

There isn't anything you've experienced or will experience with your board that doesn't fit within capacity, connection, or culture. When you nurture your board (loving it), you *can* have a board you love!

Let's get started!

CHAPTER ONE

How Do Boards Get Better?

The phone rang. It was Carlos, an executive director of a nonprofit senior housing facility. "I'm the new executive director here," he said, "and my board hasn't been engaged. I want to change that and take my board to the next level. Would you come and train them on their roles and responsibilities?"

This is typical of many calls I get. Requests like: "My board is challenged with_____" (you can no doubt fill in the blank!). What follows is a request for board member training—on roles and responsibilities, recruiting new board members, engaging the board members with fundraising, or something else.

Will training take a board to "the next level"? Will it address the challenges or create sustainable improvement? No. It's not that training, or even a day of reflection and discussion, won't contribute to board improvement; it's that training *alone* doesn't change behavior. It's not going to produce the results you and other nonprofit leaders expect, hope for, and need.

Unfortunately, training is often used to deal with an underperforming board, or even a problematic board member, with expectations that change will result.

Before we delve into the model for identifying causes of challenges with boards in upcoming chapters, learning proven practices for improving your board will arm you with the strategies you need to address them when they occur. This not only makes your life as the executive director easier, but it also matters to your nonprofit's mission. Here's how.

Why Does it Matter?

We know a nonprofit's board influences organizational performance. Although limited, research supports the relationship between an *effective* board and a nonprofit's impact. An *effective* board improves a nonprofit's performance in several areas, including organizational decision-making, strategic thinking, and attracting resources.

When your board performs well, it influences engagement with the community, invites diverse perspectives, and enhances your nonprofit's reputation and credibility. A strong board promotes positive change, sets direction, and elevates performance in achieving your nonprofit's mission.

Effective boards matter! But merely declaring it so doesn't help you achieve the board functioning level you know your nonprofit needs and deserves.

Board development is fundamentally a change process, and it's different for each nonprofit. Like any change process, it begins with an experience of dissatisfaction. Correctly diagnosing the cause of dissatisfaction—part of what this book will teach you—can make the difference between a lot of effort with little result and an efficient approach to getting the outcome you and your board want.

If you've correctly assessed the cause of a board problem, how you and your board act to make things better will determine your success. This chapter includes essential information you need about what to include in *any* solution you choose for *any* board issue, whether caused by capacity, connection, or culture.

Research

Generally, people refer to the change process of boards "getting better" as board development. Until relatively recently, we haven't had research to help nonprofit executives and board members know *how* to go about developing the board—how to catalyze it to "get better."

What Is Board Development?

Too many nonprofit leaders think board development is only recruiting, selecting, and orienting new board members. Board development is much more. It's the processes by which board members, committed to a shared mission, learn, create, and become an optimally functioning, contributing board team—ideally a diverse team rich in leadership, strategic thinking, and cultural inclusion.

Discovering the knowledge gap, I set out to explore board development more deeply by speaking with executive directors and board members who had had positive, direct experiences with it. I gathered stories of board improvement from sixty-six nonprofit leaders, supplemented with over one hundred case reviews.

Those stories revealed themes about what really happens when boards "get better," identifying three critical success factors for effective board development.

Critical Success Factors for Effective Board Development

When asked to identify the factors critical to the success of their board development efforts, regardless of what they wanted to change, almost everyone interviewed mentioned three factors:

- A nudge
- The board chair
- Intention

No one factor was more important than the others. Knowing and applying these will save time, energy, and resources when working with your board to improve or change something.

A Nudge: Outside Governance Expertise or Training

Training alone isn't going to take your board to the next level, but it can get things going. Training, particularly exposure to nonprofit governance expertise, was found to spark motivation for board change. Workshops or exposure to an outside consultant plant seeds for a new vision of what your board can be. "We recognized we could get better." "We set expectations higher." "It took someone from the outside to give us the benchmarks of a healthy board." These were typical comments.

Here's an executive's story demonstrating a nudge:

I think we had a great bunch of people on the board, but they were mostly first-timers. In retrospect, I see they didn't really know what they were supposed to be doing, so they weren't very helpful. They didn't do a good job of looking at the big picture. The board wasn't living up to its potential and didn't realize things could be different.

Then we had a full day off-site with a nonprofit governance consultant. Board members spent part of the day talking about what they should be doing and then, together, where we wanted to go. As a result, they committed to doing a self-assessment and initiated a strategic planning process. The board [members] came out of this [board development] experience way more involved, more aware of what our nonprofit does, and understanding where they could and should help.

Like Carlos in the opening story, your request for training to "take my board to the next level" is a good place to start. This is one way executive directors directly influence board development—like investing in the care and feeding of the tree. You can provide the "nudge" that results in your board's desire to improve.

The Board Chair

We know purposeful organizational change requires leadership. Findings from the stories and case review revealed that it's the board chair, *not* you, who must lead the process. No, I didn't just contradict myself. You, as the executive director, have a role. But it's not the leading role.

In every executive's story of effective board development, the board chair played a critical role in creating movement and building momentum for the change. Importantly, this was in partnership with, but not led by, the executive director. Typically, the board chair engaged a few other board members, too, building a small group of champions for change.

Representative comments include: "The board chair drove the agenda for better structure and better processes." He was "a role model" in risking a new board commitment to fundraising—the "key to our turnaround." "The president set the tone."

In contrast, Claudia, a new executive director of a housing agency, experienced her board as very involved in day-to-day operations and wanted to tackle it. Her plan was to engage board members in a board development process she hoped would focus on more strategic matters.

She realized that an effective board development process starts with a board assessment. Learning about the importance of the board chair's role, she spoke with him to gain his support.

Unfortunately, the chair didn't see any need to conduct an assessment and felt the board was too busy to take on any more "projects." "There's nothing wrong with how we're operating now," he said. Claudia realized she needed to be patient until this board chair's term was up.

Six months later, her new board chair enthusiastically embraced the project. Two years later, board members became a real asset for her by focusing on the strategic plan, no longer delving into the day-to-day operations.

The board chair has a critical role in successful board development. The interviews and case review findings indicated that it won't happen without the board chair championing change. Even in cases where areas for improvement were identified by a governance committee, the board chair's support was needed for any real progress.

Board development at its best is an ongoing process. Effective boards engage in self-assessment and identify areas for improvement. To be on target, they may need to go deeper than they think by considering board capacity, connection, and culture.

Once the real board issues and needs for improvement are identified, a good process includes prioritizing board development goals and creating a plan to achieve them. You, as the executive director, should be part of the process.

Make Your Board Chair Your Partner in Board Development

Don't be discouraged at how critical the board chair is to board development success! Your board chair is a powerful resource for you—a leadership partner who can move the board in the direction you want it to go. Of course, this will be a challenge for you if you don't have the right board chair. For this reason, you must be an integral part of an intentional process for board chair selection and board leadership development. We'll cover the board chair/executive relationship in Chapter Four, so hold tight for help with this if you need it.

Intention

As participants identified critical success factors in our interviews, the word "intention" came up repeatedly. Board development efforts work when there's a specific, articulated intention."We were obsessed with board development." "Status quo was not okay." "Yagottawanna." "We had to choose to change."

Apply these three critical success factors when you work to improve your board in any significant way: a nudge, the board chair, and intention. Knowing these helps you know what steps to take to fix the problems you assess with your new understanding of the board dimensions of capacity, connections, and culture.

Before we delve into those, there are a couple of additional points about effective board development you need to know.

Supporting Factors

In addition to the three critical success factors, three supporting factors will help you build momentum and sustain your board development effort.

A Small Change

One factor is a change, even if small, in the board's functioning or structure. When you're working with your board on improving or fixing a problem or issue, keep in mind that a small, incremental change will beget another. That builds momentum.

For example, after a training session—a nudge—one board started mission moments at each board meeting. Over time, this led to a greater understanding of their nonprofit's services, which motivated people to become more future-focused. A new strategic plan was created.

The role of the board members shifted to being more strategic. Excitement about their vision empowered more board members to step up and help with fundraising. Small steps yielded a big result for this nonprofit: a much stronger board.

Mission Moments Inspire Boards

Mission moments at a board meeting are brief and inspirational stories of how your organization's work has made a difference in the world. They could be delivered by you or another staff member, a board member, a volunteer, or even by a person whose life was changed.

These poignant examples of your organization's work inspire board members to continuously strive to make the board effective and forward-moving.

Recognition and Celebration

When I ask executive directors and board members if they've been thanked enough, no one says yes. Another factor supporting board development success is the recognition and celebration of successes. These practices fuel excitement and engagement—helping build momentum for board improvement.

One executive reported his nonprofit had experienced a severe financial crisis. A new board chair stepped up. She engaged with each individual board member to learn more. As a result, she and the executive director created a plan to focus on each person's unique way of helping, especially with expanding revenue sources. As they achieved new financial milestones, individual board members and committees were appreciated and recognized. No achievement was too small to call out. The board became much more engaged.

Team Building

As the boards in my research were changing and evolving, many were strengthening relationships among the board members and developing a sense of unity and identity as a team. Several people reported increased trust levels and improved interpersonal dynamics—all of which supported their boards' developmental process.

How Long Does It Take?

Board development is not quick. In fact, for real effectiveness, it's ongoing. The specific board development efforts reported by those interviewed took an average of four years. Really? I know; I was surprised, too.

That doesn't mean nothing changed for four years. It means, for many of the boards, needed improvements took time to be fully realized.

Frank, the executive director of a YMCA, told of their five-year board development journey. When his new board chair, Jim, was elected, he committed to doing something about a long-time goal: creating a teen center. It had been on the agenda, but *only* on the agenda, for years.

They had all wanted to increase the Y's ability to serve teens, but they didn't have the capacity, commitment, or culture on the board to achieve it. Jim realized that if they were going to achieve this ambitious goal, the board needed to be transformed.

Jim's first step was to recruit another board leader to partner with him as a change champion. They worked together to rally board members around the common goal of creating the center. Once they had a clear vision, "it was the selling point for recruiting people," Jim said.

They had to transform the board to embrace a norm of fundraising. Frank said no one resisted the idea of the teen center, but they resisted the fundraising it would require. Jim stayed the course. Over time, several board members left the board. New people came on who embraced the vision and would fundraise for it. It took two to three years to build the board with the fundraising capacity they needed. They shifted attention at meetings away from the Y's program tactics to the community engagement required to raise the money and create the center. The board evolved and developed a "new personality," according to Frank. "We built momentum in small steps." It took five years for the board changes, which ultimately resulted in making the teen center a reality.

Other, later research has found effective board development takes years. All the more reason to get started!

Nonprofit leaders have little trouble articulating what should, or could, be better about their boards. But, for successful board improvement, you need to understand what's *really* going on—what you'll learn here about capacity, connection, and culture. Keep the success factors for board development in mind to design the right approach—the "how" of positive change for your board. Consider *all three* dimensions when thinking about what you want to change to make sure you aren't leaving something important out. And come back here anytime for a refresher!

Key Lessons

- Create the nudge.
- Be intentional about board development.
- Get the board chair's buy-in.
- Be a key player in designing and participating in the board chair selection process.
- Celebrate successes and thank each other.
- To build momentum, make and acknowledge small changes.

Now we're ready to move on. In the following chapters, I'll cover the three dimensions—capacity (the tree's canopy), connections (the branches and trunk), and culture (the roots). We'll cover the people and process aspects of each as well as what to do about them, sharing what works and how to approach change for your board. Let's go!

CHAPTER TWO

Capacity: People

This time the call came from my sister. She was Master Trainer of a special developmental approach for premature babies in hospital neonatal intensive care units (NICUs). The approach engaged the mothers (often excluded from NICUs) and trained doctors and nurses in specific developmental practices. Gold standard research from Stanford Hospital, Oakland Children's Hospital, and Harvard demonstrated dramatic results from training in this approach for vulnerable premature infants.

A small group of Harvard founding psychologists formed a nonprofit to document and disseminate this model and oversee the certification process for trainers and nurseries. Let's call it the Neonatal Intervention Group (NIG). My sister was part of this founding group which comprised the board of directors. "We need help," she said. "We don't know the first thing about being a nonprofit board. We need training."

This initial board of six was focused on standards, recruiting trainers, and documentation. But they realized that to get the word out, they needed to do more than write professional articles. They needed to build the board's capacity. It needed to be much more culturally and professionally diverse to expand its reach and impact. And they needed some specific, strategic characteristics and competencies around the board table.

The NIG board members did what executive directors and board members, accurately or not, most often do: identify problems with boards as capacity issues. Executive directors typically look within what our model calls the board's capacity dimension to address challenges. And a lot of the time, it's just fine. Board capacity problems can be more easily addressed than problems rooted in your board's connection or culture dimensions. So, it makes sense to start there.

When people think of board capacity, they typically think of the people on the board and non-board members who serve on board committees. These comprise your board's people capacity. But capacity covers much more.

Your board's capacity includes its structure and the practices and processes it puts in place to get its works done efficiently and effectively. Just as your nonprofit needs to have structure and procedures for a good workflow, so does your board. Usually, the board's process capacity is built as it develops from its infancy stage to adulthood, like a tree's canopy expands as it grows. (Go to the *Resources Page* for a podcast episode on board life stages.)

The elements of your board's capacity change and expand as the board evolves—just as many trees lose leaves in the fall but then replace them and add more in the spring. Start-up nonprofits don't have everything a strong nonprofit needs at the get-go (all the people, policies, procedures, and so on), and understandably so. As nonprofits grow and mature, their boards develop more capacity.

In this chapter, we focus on your board's people capacity. We'll cover common board problems followed by what you can do about them. In the next chapter, we'll cover the board's process capacity.

Assessing Your Board's People Capacity

Issues with your board's people capacity include lack of needed skills, knowledge, diverse cultural perspectives, or abilities to lead and do the board's work. Challenges you experience with your board may just be a matter of getting the right people on it. Let's give Jim Collins credit for the metaphor: Do you have the right people on the bus? (Jim Collins, *Good to Great*, 2001. Find it on the *Resources Page.*)

This chapter explores your board's people capacity in two key areas: board composition and the executive director. Yes—you! Let's start with you.

Your Capacity as Executive Director

Having an effective board requires a significant investment of your time as the executive director. Have you been realistic with yourself about how much time it really takes? What is *your* capacity as an executive director?

Your capacity is an integral component of your board's people capacity because you, as the executive director, are such a critical player on the board team. I'm not suggesting you be an elected board member. In fact, I don't recommend it. But you work in such close collaboration with all the board members in a variety of ways. Your capacity matters to the board, and I'm arguing it's essential to your board's performance.

I advise executives to plan for at least 20 percent of their time working on or with the board—and that's a minimum. It can and, if you're able, should be more. While you're doing a strategic plan, for example, the demands on your time with the board could easily top 25 to 30 percent.

Wait! I know. I hear your objections: "How can I possibly give that much time to the board? They're supposed to be an asset, not a drain." Remember, you are part of the leadership team for your nonprofit, along with your board. If you have a staff management or executive team, I bet you wouldn't think it surprising to spend over 20 percent of your time each week supporting them and their success. (Check out the "It Starts at the Top" podcast episode on the *Resources Page*.)

Ever eat lunch at your desk or in your car? Work late more than occasionally—to the point where working ten-hour days is the norm? Work on a weekend? Ever feel guilty saying no to a request for your time and attention? Or worse, are you saying yes most of the time?

Believe me, I know. I did all of this when I was an executive director. I hope you're beginning to see why you must safeguard and build your own capacity. And, I'm absolutely sure, when you invest your time with your board, you'll reap benefits beyond what you think or hope for. Your investment in your board will make your work even more rewarding and free you up in ways you can't now imagine.

Your ability to nudge and support your board to take advantage of the insights, tips, and strategies in this book depends on your capacity. Remember, your board's people capacity includes you.

What to Do About It: Develop, Nurture, and Safeguard Your Own Capacity

I can't say enough how important it is for you as the executive director to nurture, develop, and closely guard your own capacity. I've experienced executive directors who seem to be proud of overworking. Being a martyr to your mission will not result in a good outcome—for you or for your nonprofit.

To effectively manage your capacity and enhance your productivity—and thus results for your board and your nonprofit—you need to commit to renewal. We know spending more time doesn't mean you'll get better results. You're not more productive because you're busier.

See if this sounds familiar: Jane is working twelve to fourteen hours a day in and on her nonprofit. She feels exhausted a lot and finds it difficult to engage with her husband and children when she gets home in the evenings. As a result, she feels guilty and dissatisfied. She doesn't sleep well, makes no time for exercise, and eats on the run or at her desk.

You and I both know Jane's experience is not uncommon.

Research found employees who learned and used practices to build their personal energy (capacity) out-performed employees who didn't but worked more hours. (Swartz, T. and McCarthy, C., "Manage Your Energy, Not Your Time," *Harvard Business Review*, October 2007.) Working more hours is not productive. The problem with working more hours is time is finite. No matter how hard you work, you can't create more time.

But energy is different. To increase your effectiveness and productivity, you need to master renewal: manage your energy, not your time. Studies show energy renewal practices actually increase productivity. You *can* increase your energy.

There are four dimensions of personal energy: physical, emotional, mental, and spiritual. We build our energy by fostering simple rituals in our lives. You can build your energy through renewal practices within each of the four dimensions. I highlight some of the particularly effective renewal practices for you here. These aren't new. I'm sure you've heard of them. What I want you to do is "hear" them now through the lens of your new insights about their implications for you personally.

Be forewarned: this will seem counterintuitive because energy renewal practices mean you take time away from work. But study after study shows this works. In one, using energy renewal practices, employees of a bank got much better results (per the bank's metrics) than their colleagues who didn't.

Here are some practices within each personal energy dimension for you to consider. They work. Choose from these or create your own. But do *something!*

1. Physical energy renewal practices include getting more sleep, reducing alcohol use, exercising, and taking breaks. Some examples to help you do something in this dimension are to go to bed earlier or set an alarm to sound every hour and then spend five minutes moving around.

26

2. Emotional energy renewal practices may not be as obvious. One I find helpful is to practice gratitude. (Being grateful throughout the day—noticing even small things you're thankful for—will increase your positive emotions.) Keep a gratitude journal on your nightstand, and, every night, write down five things you're grateful for.

3. Another way to build your emotional energy is to take the long view in upsetting situations. For example, ask yourself if what's happening will matter to you in a year. In five years. Another tip is to look for the lesson in any situation when you feel down or just emotionally tired. Doing that can shift your mindset and give you more energy.

4. Mental energy renewal practices include reducing distractions in places you work and even at home. For example, look around your office and evaluate if what you see supports your ability to focus or instead distracts you. If the latter, remove it. Another suggestion is to avoid taking your phone into meetings. And, don't multitask! We know it drains your mental energy.

5. Spiritual energy renewal practices may not have come to mind at all. Ways to build yours include doing more of the activities you love and delegating tasks you like the least. Another way to build spiritual energy is to identify what you value most and use those values to guide your choices.

It's important: choose renewal practices and get them in your calendar. Make time for what matters. You may *think* taking care of yourself and working less matters. But what really counts is what you *do* about it.

Your personal capacity matters when it comes to having an effective board. I hope you see how and are motivated to do something about it. The canopy of a tree is incomplete without a variety of leaves. Just like leaves for the canopy, you're a crucial part of your board's people capacity.

Now let's explore problems that show up in the second key area of your board's people capacity, board composition.

Your Board's Composition

Board composition is about having the right people and enough of them. You've no doubt heard that executive directors need board members who bring "time, talent, and treasure." Board people capacity includes:

- Time—enough board members who show up and get work done;
- Talent—having the right people with the characteristics your board needs for impact; and
- Treasure—board members who contribute or fundraise.

Let's look at the predictable problems you may experience with each of these and what you can do about them.

Not Having Enough People

Board challenges with people capacity include not having enough people. I get asked often: How many people should we have on our board? Well, it depends.

First, know what your state, province, or equivalent jurisdiction requires. You don't want your board to violate the law. In my state, California, every board needs three directors—not many! I don't recommend it as your goal. There's such a thing as a board that's too small.

I was on the phone with a founding executive director who was overwhelmed and totally stressed. She and her husband founded this nonprofit start-up to train people who experienced trauma to help other trauma victims heal and build resilience. The program was growing, and she was busy training trainers to deliver it.

They had the required minimum three-person board. Evaluations showed great program results, so they were poised to grow. Their growing nonprofit, and their small board, needed a lot. This executive was torn among multiple demands to get donors, write grants, create a strategic plan, recruit volunteers, and manage the US and Africa programs.

And she needed more board members to build social capital and a culturally diverse board, focus lean resources, network for fundraising, and support her. Her board members were doing what they could, but three just wasn't enough.

Not Having the Right People

Having the people capacity you need is not just a matter of having enough people on your board. You need the *right* people.

The executive director and board chair of a nonprofit community theatre reported numerous efforts to increase board fundraising. They had had many discussions about the characteristics of the people they should recruit. Being in the high-tech Silicon Valley in California, one board member suggested they get someone from Google, Facebook, or Apple. He argued that a corporate connection on their board would open many doors, attract corporate money, and lead to relationships with wealthy people.

No one on the board, or the staff for that matter, had any links to these companies. There was a lot of talk and ideas, but no action. After many fruitless board discussions about the "type" of people to recruit, they began instead to explore more deeply why past efforts with people of influence, with whom they did have contacts, hadn't gotten the results they expected.

They realized what they needed was a fundraising leader— someone who was confident about where and how to begin with board members inexperienced in fundraising—more than they needed someone with deep pockets or influential connections. Recognizing this gap in leadership capacity made all the difference. They focused on recruiting a fundraising leader, found someone, and a year later had an empowered and effective fund development committee raising more money than ever.

Another people-capacity problem arises when the people on your board lack the needed critical governing competencies. I often hear executive directors lament that their board members don't know their governing roles and responsibilities. Everyone on the board needs basic competencies and knowledge about "doing" governance effectively.

Here's another example of a board composition people-capacity problem. Have you ever experienced a board where financial literacy is limited to the treasurer? Everyone defers to the treasurer, trusting the treasurer's approval or recommendation is based on sound financials. This may be

---

Your Role versus the Board's Role

Executive directors need to understand the distinction between their role and the board's, too. A principle you can use is remembering governing (the board's job) never includes managing your nonprofit's day-to-day operations—that's your job. It may not be so black and white in practice, but this is the understanding you all need to have.

---

true, but each individual board member who votes must do so "independently," which requires at least a basic understanding of the financial statements. (There's a link to a good book for this on the *Resources Page*.)

Another board composition problem is a scarcity of leaders on the board. This comes up when no one is willing to be an officer or committee chair. Or maybe you lack board members with the leadership skills to do so effectively. Not everyone on the board is or should be a leader, but on many boards, this is a real gap.

No discussion of people capacity on boards would be complete without acknowledging the importance of board diversity, culturally or otherwise. Lack of board diversity is a pervasive problem in our sector. We know over 80 percent of the people serving on nonprofit boards in the United States are Caucasian. If your board is not diverse, it *may* be a people-capacity problem. I say *may* be because lack of diversity is not just about seats at the table.

It's fundamentally about inclusion. Without commitment and intentional focus on diversity, equity, and inclusion, you won't get a great board. Equity and inclusion are elements of your board's culture. In my experience, the reasons nonprofit boards are not diverse are rooted in values, mindsets, and other aspects of your board's culture. I have more to say about board diversity throughout the book, particularly in the chapter on culture, the third dimension of your board in our model.

What to Do About It: Effectively Recruit and Orient Board Members

You need a robust board recruitment *system* and its partner, an effective board orientation program, to address the people-capacity problems with board composition we've discussed. *Effective* board recruitment and orientation will get the right people in the right seats—and enough of them. Board recruitment and orientation are critical components of your board's process capacity, so we'll cover them in the next chapter.

But building your board's people capacity requires more. Here are some other things to do to ensure you have the right board members, and enough of them.

What to Do About It: Align Board Composition with Strategic Goals

Agreement on the answer to this question defines your nonprofit's strategic goals: "If we are very successful in advancing our mission in the near future, say, three years out, what results will we achieve?" Those results—your agreed-upon strategic goals—set the direction and priorities for you and your board.

Is your board's composition driven by those goals? Do the skills, talents, and characteristics of board members match what is needed for your board to get *its work* done to achieve those goals, for example, fundraising, advocacy, facility development, and oversight?

To align your board composition with your strategic goals, your board needs to determine if there is *governing* work needed to achieve each goal. (Get a handout on the *Resources Page*.) (This is a discussion I encourage you and your board to have once you've agreed on the goals. Doing this should be a natural part of your board's work, but I rarely see it.)

Often after a planning process, board members look to the executive director as if to say: "It's all yours now." Sound familiar? Doing what I recommend here will change that.

You do have a role with your board in this situation. Help your board chair lead a discussion, so your board members recognize the opportunities they have, within governing, to help achieve the strategic goals.

Once your board agrees on the results it will work to achieve, the stage is set for evaluating and aligning your board's composition. In partnership with your board chair, help your board decide: How will we achieve those results? Who will do what, and who will lead the work?

As you answer the "who" question, the gaps in your board's people capacity become clear. Maybe you don't have the people capacity you need to do the board's work, whether what's missing is enough people, the right competencies or characteristics, or both.

Consider the NIG. It had an inspiring vision: changing the future of babies in intensive care. But beyond implementing its approach in NICU training protocols throughout the world, it didn't have strategic goals to advance its mission.

So, it completed a planning process to develop those goals. Next, it tackled the role of the board and its work. As leaders considered how they would do the board's work, they realized they needed different competencies and connections. They discovered they needed marketing, communications, and finance expertise. They found they needed parents' perspectives and engagement on the board, not just in the hospital.

With your board members, thoughtfully consider what expertise, knowledge, and connections you need on the board to achieve your nonprofit's strategic goals. And, if you have gaps, be intentional and fill them.

To have the board you want and deserve, with the people capacity needed for effectiveness, be sure you and your board align the board's composition with your strategic goals.

More to Do about People Capacity: Ensure You Have Leaders on Your Board

Leadership as a board member characteristic is so important. There are many characteristics you have, need, and want among board members, but leadership deserves special attention. Ensuring you have board *leaders* is essential for building your board's people capacity. Many boards don't even consider it until a glaring lack creates a crisis.

Ever heard of a board with no one to step up as the board chairperson? Or a board without anyone *qualified* to step into that critical leadership role? The stories you've heard are, unfortunately, true. National research surveying board chairs and other board leaders confirms it. (Go to the *Resources Page* for a copy of the study report.)

Governance *is* leadership. Your board's responsibility is to advance your nonprofit's mission in collaboration with you. And that requires leadership. Your board needs leaders to fulfill these four functions:

- Envision the future;
- Know reality and respond;
- Inspire and engage others to act; and
- Self-reflect and self-manage.

Observe and assess the leadership capacity of your board. Think about the board members you have with these functions in mind. If you don't have board members who personally embody these functions (or enough of them), work with your board to add leadership to board member recruitment criteria. Let's look a little closer at the four leadership functions you need.

Four Leadership Functions Your Board Needs

1. Leaders envision a better future. This is one of the ways board members have an impact. The board can be a catalyst for change. There are many appropriate governing roles within this leadership function. For example, as a result of planning, you and your board may decide to review the mission or explore a strategic partnership.

2. Leaders realize to create a better future, they must be realistic about their starting point. Another board leadership function is to know reality and respond. Board members need to understand the current state of your nonprofit and the environment in which it operates. Their ability to do so is part of your board's people capacity.

There's a natural tension your board members need to manage: the tension between aspiring to create more and being grounded in the reality of what is and what it will take to get there. Let me give you an example:

> A nonprofit serving high-risk youth hired a new executive director, Mai. The group focused for years on serving youth in one geographic location. Their services demonstrated a strong success rate getting these youth through high school and into college. Mai could see the potential of bringing their proven approach into a neighboring county.

> The board chair was excited to partner with her to present this opportunity to the board. They had no funding to cover the costs of replicating the program, and several board members couldn't support it as a result. Rather than commit to seeking ways to make it happen, they got stuck in the "yes, but" thinking of the board members who could only see the limits of their situation. The opportunity was put on hold.

Mai and her board chair worked together to attract community leaders to the board over the next few years. They made leadership a criterion for new board members. The board composition changed, and the opportunity was revisited. Mai had the leaders on the board she needed to establish their program in a new community. When the leadership capacity of the board shifted, a better future was possible.

I share this story so you can see how the characteristics of board members as leaders play out. Those who are stuck in current realities and dismiss new ideas too quickly don't serve your nonprofit. You need a healthy number of board members who can see reality *and* hold a vision to create the greatest impact.

3. The third leadership function is to inspire and engage others to act. Your board members are uniquely positioned to leverage their networks and be a bridge to your community. The ability to be an effective ambassador and advocate is a board member characteristic—and part of a board's people capacity—you can't afford to be without. Be intentional in recruiting board members with the ability and willingness to articulate, outside the boardroom, your mission and its impact.

4. The final leadership function your board needs to fulfill is something you may not have thought of before: the ability and willingness to self-reflect and self-manage. Effective leaders are self-aware. They use self-reflection to learn and adapt—managing themselves in the situations they encounter.

Board members are responsible for developing themselves and for working together to develop the board as an effective team. Your board members' capacity to self-reflect and self-manage requires openness to assessing themselves and to learning.

Anita, the board chair of a hospital auxiliary, called to request help with the board. She recently stepped into this leadership role after serving on the board for several years. After discussion, it became clear I could best assist by helping Anita and the board conduct a board self-assessment—a structured way for board members to reflect on how they were doing and what could be better.

Upon presenting this opportunity, Anita got quite a bit of pushback from board members. She told me a couple of board members felt their "toes were stepped on" by her suggesting there could be anything they needed to learn about how they were doing. Unlike Anita, several others failed to see the value in reflection and learning. They felt an assessment wouldn't be useful and that they needed to focus on other things.

This is an example of a lack of board leadership. Anita alone was not enough. The opportunity for this board to strengthen itself as an effective, contributing team was lost.

I hope you see that the amount and quality of leadership among your board members is a critical element of your board's people capacity. Use this functional framework to assess leadership on your board.

Many board problems are the result of not having the right people on your board or enough of them. I encourage you to pause for a moment and consider: do you have the type and amount of individual and collective people capacity on your board for optimal performance and impact?

Another Board Composition Problem: Board Members Do Too Little or Too Much

People capacity on boards is not just about having the right people. It doesn't matter how many board members you have if they aren't doing what you need them to do. The time your board members give can be too little to be effective. Or, it can be too much, with a few board members overcommitting—doing all the work. I've seen this cause other board members to step back, disengaged.

If those doing too much don't burn out, your nonprofit is still vulnerable. You have all your eggs in one basket! It's a people-capacity problem when you and your board members aren't clear about the time each has to devote to your nonprofit or the amount doesn't match your needs and expectations.

Have you ever had a board retreat at which everyone gets fired up, an inspiring idea develops, and people are eager to work on it? Then, not too long after, the momentum slows? It happened to Antonia.

Antonia was the executive director of the HMV Foundation. The foundation was established to select and raise money for special school projects the local public high school's limited budget could not address. Its nine-member board was comprised mostly of parents.

Before the retreat, board members were getting bogged down in the operational details of choosing the projects to fund and how those projects should be implemented. But, for the first time, the board members established a three-year strategic vision at the retreat. They agreed that to have more mission impact, they needed to focus on community engagement—helping nonparents in their community see the value of supporting the school.

They agreed to create a new board committee to develop a plan. Then they reviewed all their committees and who was leading or serving on each. When they came to the new community engagement committee, no one stepped up. The board members could see what they were already committed to, and no one had the personal capacity to take on more. The goal to increase community engagement was dropped. As a result, they weren't able to increase nonparent engagement with, and support for, the school.

Overcommitment is a personal issue for board members. Your board has a people-capacity issue if any board members are stretching themselves too thin.

What to Do About It: Negotiate and Acknowledge Board Members' Personal Capacity

Have a frank conversation individually with board members—ideally when they are first recruited and annually after that—about the personal resources, time, talent, and treasure they can and will bring to board service. This should happen in an in-person meeting with you (as the executive director) and your board chair. Or it may be the chair of the governance committee—whatever works for you. The important thing is to do this!

One executive director I know called this practice a game-changer for her and her board (there's a link to her podcast episode on the *Resources Page*). Encourage board members to be realistic about their personal capacity and not overcommit. Your ongoing, personalized support and appreciation are critical to unleashing the full potential of each board member. You don't want untapped capacity on your board!

These meetings are one way you invest your time—the 20 percent-plus we talked about—in the board. They'll help you and your board assess if people are in the right seats, identify gaps in the board's composition, and see opportunities to expand its capacity.

Term Limits

I recommend board member term limits. For example, a board member serves two to three terms and then is required to rotate off the board for at least one year. Having term limits helps you communicate clearly about board member commitments and opens opportunities for new relationships.

Your Board Members Don't Fundraise

Does your board need "treasure" in its people capacity? Whether or not you need board members to fundraise depends on your nonprofit's financial model. Your board's people capacity may need to include people willing to give, people who have personal resources, or people who have connections to resources.

If fundraising is a revenue source for your nonprofit, your board needs to be involved with it. You can't expect others to give to your nonprofit if board members don't—it's as if they're telling the community your nonprofit doesn't need the money, it doesn't matter, or worse, it doesn't deserve it. And it's not about how much to give. When board members—key leaders of your nonprofit—won't invest even a small amount in your mission, why should anyone else?

What to Do About It: Empower Your Board to Fundraise

If you're transitioning a board from nonfundraising to fundraising, work with your board to do these three things:

- Help board members start small but establish new expectations for current board members about fundraising.
- Create criteria related to fundraising for new board members you'll recruit.
- Develop or recruit board members who can and will lead board fundraising. I'm not talking about making a significant gift themselves, although that would be nice. I'm talking about a few key leaders who can mentor, coach, and encourage fellow board members to find a comfortable starting point and take the first step.

We know from research 90 percent of a board member's fundraising role is identifying, cultivating, and stewarding relationships—not making the ask. Make sure your board members understand this. I've found many board members resist fundraising because they don't want to ask people for money. They need to understand there are many ways they can help without having to make the ask. (There's a guide on the *Resources Page*.)

How your board members think about fundraising may be rooted in assumptions or a mindset that gets in the way.

Attitudes about fundraising are part of your board's culture, and we'll be covering those in Chapter Six.

Your Board Members Don't Understand Their Governing Roles

Some people-capacity problems stem from a lack of knowledge. One problem with boards I hear about a lot from executive directors (and board members) is board members being too involved with day-to-day operations. They just don't understand what it means to govern, which is a people-capacity issue.

What to Do About It: Provide Effective Board Education

Board people-capacity challenges can be addressed by training—building board members' knowledge is one way to build your board's capacity. Ensure board members understand the distinctions between staff roles (managing and working in day-to-day operations) and governing.

An all-volunteer nonprofit museum had a board mostly focused on the daily operations. With seven board members, they recognized that to grow and advance their mission, they needed to evolve. The board president, who was functioning more as an executive director, approached me for help.

With a couple of other board members, our small group designed a board retreat agenda, integrating board education and action planning. The retreat kicked off with an informative session, a governance "refresher" about the board's importance and functions, how it contributes to advancing the mission, and how governing the museum is distinct from managing it.

Board members were asked to reflect on how this knowledge applied to them. Together they shared their preferences and responses to their new understanding of what it means to govern. They adopted and implemented an action plan that included an agreement to individually select a volunteer "staff" role, a board member role, or both—if they could manage both—by the next board meeting.

They decided to restructure their meetings. They would first meet as the board. They would then adjourn and convene as a leadership council focusing on museum operations and management. They engaged me to coach them to put an effective board recruitment system in place and adopt a board orientation program. (Learn more on the *Resources Page*.)

Within four months, they recruited and oriented three new governing board members, all of whom matched their strategic goals. And they built momentum. Once the new board members were in place, members of the board who only wanted to do "staff" work resigned from the board but remained on the active leadership council.

Tips for Making It Stick

Training rarely changes behavior. But the above example highlights how board education can kick off a process that truly builds board capacity. It is often the nudge we discussed in Chapter One. Keep in mind: people need to apply and use knowledge for it to stick. If training is your chosen

[handwritten margin note: Board vs. leadership council!]

intervention, be sure you build some key features into your approach, so it's effective.

Here are four tips:

1. Facilitate participants' engagement with the information being provided, so the content links to them personally in some way.
2. Design the training to address the different learning styles. You can search the web for ideas.
3. Give assignments as part of your training, so participants have ways to apply what they've learned, both in the training session and afterward.
4. Be sure there are agreements about the implications of the board's training, if applicable, and next steps.

These suggestions are relevant for any area you feel can be addressed by board education, like financial literacy or understanding deeply your programs and services.

A final tip for effective board education is to evaluate its impact. Did you get the desired result? Did it last? The board problem you think is a people-capacity issue to be resolved with training may be an issue with connection or culture. If you evaluate the results from training, you'll learn if the board problem is in one of the other dimensions.

Key Lessons

- Nurture your own capacity.
- Recruit board members using an effective *system*.
- Align board composition with strategic goals.
- Recruit and develop board leaders.

- Educate board members, including that governance *is* leadership.
- Understand each board member's capacity.
- Use the tips for making board education stick.

Wrapping It Up

Problems experienced with boards aren't always complex. Sometimes they're simply a matter of capacity. I don't mean to imply capacity issues are all easy. Still, in my experience, they are understood more quickly, and the solutions are often more apparent than with other board challenges. The leaves of our tree's canopy are right out in the open for us to see.

In this chapter, we covered the people aspect of board capacity and the issues you may experience with your board about the people you have, or don't have, on the board—your board composition. And I called out how important *you* are as a member of the board team—a critical part of your board's people capacity.

We explored the people capacity of your board and common problems fitting in this part of the model and action steps to address them, including self-care for you.

Boards' people capacity cannot be addressed in a vacuum. It's interdependent with the other dimensions: connection and culture. As you've already seen with the interplay of board people capacity and board recruitment, your board's people capacity is influenced by and integrated with its process capacity. In many cases, problems with people capacity can be solved by turning your attention to the other element of capacity: process.

The process capacity of your board is what we're going to explore next. Come with me to Chapter Three.

CHAPTER THREE

Capacity: Process

Rosa sounded scared. "What if I end up without any board members?" She was down to three and about to lose another one. And, they had no process in place for, or any idea how to start, recruiting. More questions revealed Rosa had basically been running her youth science education nonprofit without any board engagement.

When Rosa joined her nonprofit about three years before connecting with me, she had come from the high-tech industry in Silicon Valley. She didn't know the roles and responsibilities of a board—her small board (at the time, five people) didn't either. The prior executive director had recruited a rubber-stamp board. After his departure, by some miracle, they found Rosa but stopped doing much else.

Rosa not only had a people-capacity problem with her board. They also lacked any effective board processes, e.g., rarely meeting, having no officers, and being out of compliance with the bylaws. Even though this nonprofit was over fifteen years old, they were just like a start-up with the obligatory minimum of three board members and nothing else established by or for the board.

Your board's process capacity includes the structure, practices, and policies it has in place to get its work done efficiently and effectively. These are like additional leaves in a tree's canopy. Healthy trees have lush, robust canopies.

Board process capacity includes board meetings and how they're managed. It also includes board committees and how they get the board's work done.

Board process capacity includes board policies. Problems with the board may result from not having the necessary policies to either comply with regulations relevant to your nonprofit or guide board decisions and actions effectively.

Your board's process capacity is also about having effective practices to get the right work done efficiently. Problems arise when your board doesn't have consistent ways of accomplishing its work. I refer to these consistent ways of doing things as *systems*—sets of interrelated practices for getting something done. Board member recruitment, orientation, board self-assessment, and the executive director evaluation process are examples.

Does your board have the structure, policies, practices, and systems in place to facilitate its essential work and fulfill its governance responsibilities? We will address these below, starting with board structure.

A critical point: you have a role in all of this! A board lacking process capacity is ineffective and inefficient, and you're directly impacted, as is your nonprofit. As you read on, you may feel the suggestions are for the board members to implement. Yes, but. You can be the nudge for change. Ask questions, make suggestions, share the insights you're gaining here. You indeed have a role, and real influence, in transforming your board.

Challenges with board structure show up in board meetings and committees, including ad hoc committees or task forces.

Your Board's Meetings

How your board functions largely plays out during its meetings. Problems rooted in all three dimensions—capacity, connection, and culture—are likely to manifest in some way during board meetings. The structure of how your board gets its work done is part of your board's process capacity.

Some problems with board meetings are more serious than others. Here are issues with board meetings caused by a lack of board process capacity:

- Lack of meeting preparation. Failure to provide premeeting materials on time or meetings consumed by reports board members could read in advance.
- Getting and keeping a quorum. The board can't fulfill its responsibilities if it can't act, and it certainly can't achieve its potential to advance your mission.
- Not having a clear agenda to guide the board meeting flow and highlight the actions needed can be the cause of inefficient board meetings.

51

- Board meetings being dominated by a few people or lengthy discussions and no action. This can be caused by a board chair who doesn't know how to manage a meeting or use an agenda.
- Board meetings may be overly focused on day-to-day operations, and you may be micromanaged. Perhaps your board hasn't defined its roles and work in achieving your nonprofit's strategic goals. This is a common reason boards focus too much on operational issues in meetings. Are your board members spending more time on your job than theirs?
- Sometimes issues voted on in a previous meeting resurface, and the board struggles to move forward. Revisiting old issues may be caused by a lack of good board meeting minutes. This could be caused by a failure to review minutes for completeness or errors or failure to even read them.
- Board meetings may be too infrequent, e.g., quarterly. If people miss a quarterly meeting, how can they effectively participate in decisions after a more than six-month absence? And less-frequent meetings can result in an overactive executive committee or decisions made by the executive or the board chair between meetings.
- On the other hand, too-frequent meetings can be a deterrent to attracting the people you need and want because they're too busy to attend.

Here's an experience I had with a board lacking good process capacity. A friend of mine was the board chair of a women's business association, an all-volunteer nonprofit. She approached me and shared their need for nonprofit expertise to help with one of their strategic goals. She asked if I would consider joining the board, and I did.

I showed up for my first meeting. The agenda consisted of committee reports. The chair of each committee proceeded to tell us all what was worked on since the last board meeting. There were questions, but none of the committees needed the board to decide anything. They weren't even asking for board members' advice.

Even worse, I learned they had a running list of all the items "left over" from prior meetings.

The meeting was scheduled to last two hours. After two and a half hours, I needed to leave. Their problems with board productivity and meeting management were the result of a lack of board process capacity.

What to Do About It: Create Productive Board Meetings

Board members, individually and collectively, take action to advance your mission in many ways. Still, a board *meeting* is a consistent process involving *all* board members and is critical to board performance. Board meetings need to produce results advancing your nonprofit's mission and keeping board members engaged, bringing their best selves in service. The purpose of board meetings is to make decisions advancing the mission of your nonprofit.

Productive board meetings are an essential component of your board's process capacity. The key factors influencing board meeting quality, efficiency, and board member engagement are meeting frequency and duration, prep work, agendas, meeting content, facilitation, and follow-up. Here's what each of those entails and some tips for making them work for you.

Board Meeting Frequency and Duration

I get asked all the time: How often should our board meet? Most boards in the United States meet monthly. I'm sure there are very effective boards meeting less often—every other month, quarterly.

Meeting frequency should be driven by purpose derived from your mission and from a clear recognition—on your part and board members' parts—of how an effective board is an important strategic asset. Don't underutilize it.

I've seen many times that even very busy people want to invest in a mission and attend monthly meetings as long as they're interesting and purposeful.

Good board meetings support the efficient use of time. They're not too long. Maybe you're thinking: "Well, how long should a board meeting be?" Good question. The perhaps not-so-satisfying answer is, "It depends."

The length of your board meetings should be determined by what needs to get done. Make time for meaningful discussions when needed. Sometimes, you may want or need a longer session, such as at a board retreat or half-day strategic planning meeting. Sometimes, your agenda will be short. In those cases, evaluate whether you need to meet at all.

Board Meeting Prep Work: Committees and the Board Packet

Efficient boards use committees to delve into the questions and action items with which the board is engaged. With committees doing the data gathering, exploring key questions, and doing the detailed work needed for the board to make an important decision, the board is freed to focus on strategic and other important issues at its meetings.

Committee work is foundational for a good board meeting. The work done by committees is part of your board's process capacity. It's related to productive board meetings but also the effectiveness of your board overall. We'll talk more about committees and their special role in your board's process capacity below.

It's your job as executive director to ensure your board members have the information they need to consider critical questions and make sound decisions. The board packet is one tool for you to use. Others include presentations, professional expert guests, and stakeholder participants, for example. Be sure you have a consensus about how much in advance you should send the board packet.

Board members' legal duty of care requires them to exercise care in governing. There's a summary of board member legal duties on the *Resources Page*. This means preparing for meetings—thoroughly reviewing information and materials, such as items in your board packet, received in a reasonable time.

Every board member is unique, and information needs will vary from member to member. Your job as executive director will be easier if you discuss how much detail you need to provide with your board members. Your goal is for them to agree *as a whole* on this, so you don't have different individuals making multiple asks of you. This can be done by discussing it at a full board meeting where members agree on particular guidelines for you, including the type, amount, and timing for sharing the desired information in the board packet. After some experience, you'll get a feel for how much is enough.

Committee work and the board packet's content and timeliness are vital elements of your board's process capacity.

Board Meeting Agendas

How the content of board meetings is prioritized and timed is outlined in the board meeting agenda. A good agenda also identifies the action required for each item.

National research on board chairs found most board agendas are created by the board chair and the executive director together. (The study summary is on the *Resources Page*.) If not true for you, work with your board chair to make it happen. Then, by influencing what gets on the agenda, you're able to promote the board's focus on strategic issues.

Members of an executive director roundtable, which met monthly at lunchtime, discussed their boards and board meetings. One member, Lorena, the executive director of a local animal shelter, was clearly excited to share a change she experienced with her board. After their three-year strategic plan was adopted, Lorena worked with her board chair, Nina, to reevaluate the board meeting agendas. Nina was an experienced board chair and suggested they adopt something she used with another nonprofit: a board agenda structured with the strategic goals in mind.

Those items on the agenda looked something like this:

(4:05) Strategic goal #1—Expand services to a new county
Related agenda items:

a. Board input to executive director about a key related question and staffing implication

b. Discussion and decision on recommendation brought by the board task force working on the goal.

After moving away from a more traditional agenda featuring regular committee and staff reports, not only was there more progress on their strategic goals, board members were more engaged, and few missed meetings. Discussions were interesting and sometimes challenging but consistently productive.

A consent agenda is an instrumental component of your board's process capacity your board should be using. It's one agenda item grouping together other items requiring a board vote but not discussion. Examples are meeting minutes, financial reports requiring approval, approval of a contract, or a lease renewal reviewed and vetted at a previous meeting. The consent agenda is voted on all at once, usually at the beginning of the meeting. Any board member may request an item on the consent agenda be removed for discussion.

Any minutes or reports on the consent agenda should 1) require board action and 2) be distributed ahead of the meeting to give board members time to review them thoroughly and come to the meeting prepared to vote.

Effective board meetings are an essential part of your board's process capacity. We have three more factors influencing board meeting quality, efficiency, and board member engagement to cover: meeting content, facilitation, and follow-up.

Board Meeting Content

The core of your board's meetings is the content it focuses on. Ideally, it focuses on crucial strategic work and its ongoing work such as oversight and performance assessment. The primary focus of board meeting content should be discussion items requiring board member input or decisions.

If your board is overly focused on *your* work—day-to-day operations—make it a priority to support its transition away from it. I know; it's easier said than done. But if the problem belongs here—within the board's process capacity—there are some things you can put into place to help pretty quickly.

Your board's focus on operations may be the result of its developmental stage. (Check out the podcast episode on board life stages on the *Resources Page*.) Building your board's capacity is sometimes about facilitating its growing up. Young boards are often comprised of friends or relatives of the founder who come on the board to fulfill the legal requirements or set up and operate the new nonprofit, serving as unpaid staff.

Those board members (who could be the majority) may focus on operations. A tip to ensure effective *governing* meeting content is to clearly separate strategic and governing issues and decisions from operational ones. I gave an example of this earlier. Convene the board for governing and adjourn when governing work is done. Reconvene, if needed, as a management team, working on the day-to-day. Do this so the board doesn't lose sight of its *governing* role.

If your nonprofit is not young and you have a challenge with a board too focused on day-to-day work, here are some additional tips:

- Ensure your board has a consistent and complete orientation and board members clearly understand their governing roles and responsibilities.
- If the board members are overstepping their boundaries, assert yourself as the executive director. You can do this diplomatically—remind them "that" is not their job.
- Identify two or three board members who are clear about their roles and ask them to be proactive in speaking up when board meeting discussions are going awry this way.
- Partner with your board chair to keep the board out of operations at its meetings. If you see operational questions on board meeting agendas or your board slips into those discussions off the agenda, work with your board chair to change it. If you must, implement the management team meeting strategy described above but only as a time-limited, transitional strategy.

Evaluate board meeting content with your strategic goals in mind but also your mission. (We discussed mission moments earlier—use them!) Oversight is important, but effective board meetings include, from time to time, opportunities for board members to engage in meaningful discussions—perhaps about values, complex strategic questions, and challenges you want board members to help you sort out.

You'll also want to occasionally take time during board meetings for board development—education or activities to help the board be more effective.

Board Meeting Facilitation and Follow-up

Facilitation is critical. It's how the board chair, or whoever is leading the meeting, leads it. Nothing influences a board meeting more than the board chair. Your board chair must understand the role, and the core of the role is facilitation. (There's a board chair job description on the *Resources Page*.)

The chair of a board I was on clearly thought it was her job to be sure everyone was heard. She didn't want to offend anyone, so she let people go on and on. She didn't know how to diplomatically move the agenda forward or help the board create and abide by ground rules focused on action and discussion. She was open to coaching on this point from a recommended consultant. Once she knew what to do differently, everything changed. Meetings moved forward, and she gained the confidence she needed to limit discussion appropriately.

Once the board meeting is over, follow-up includes ensuring meeting minutes are completed, distributed, and amended as needed; supporting committee work; and communication. You, with the board, determine who does what between the board meetings.

Board Meetings: Executive Sessions

An executive session is a board meeting (or portion thereof) called for a purpose other than the regular board meeting. It generally is held as part of a regular board meeting, usually at the end.

But this is where it starts to get more complicated. Some would argue executive sessions, by definition, are exclusive to board members. This is not always true in practice. Board executive sessions can include executive directors except when the issue discussed is directly about them.

Some are convened for the board to discuss important organizational issues *with* the executive director but are characterized by excluding anyone else, such as the development director or CFO. Individuals with special information (your auditor or an attorney) may be invited to attend.

Depending on how they're handled, board meeting executive sessions cause trouble for the executive director. For example, if a board doesn't regularly hold executive sessions and then calls one, except for handling executive director performance evaluation or compensation discussions, it can trigger anxiety for the executive director.

I've heard executives complain they don't know what is being discussed and are concerned the board members don't have the crucial information they need. Or executives suspect the board is discussing them but don't know for sure, and the board chair doesn't share anything about what went on during the session.

You no doubt have your own experience and opinions about board executive sessions.

What to Do About It: Create a Policy for Executive Sessions

I recommend every board work with its executive director to establish a transparent process and guidelines for calling and convening executive sessions. This is part of your board's process capacity like any other board policy. The procedures should be in writing and address who attends, relevant topics, the process for calling it, and how decisions will be communicated—especially to the executive director.

Every board is unique, and whatever the process is for getting on the agenda could serve as the means for calling an executive session. Who attends is the key issue—it's the defining characteristic of an executive session—and should be based on the purpose.

There are no set rules. Examples include:

- Discussion of the executive director's performance and compensation;
- Handling matters presenting some liability or risk to the organization, which should then include the executive;
- Figuring out how to respond to a serious complaint about a board member; or
- Simply enhancing board communication and cohesion as a group.

This is an element of your board's process capacity—create it if you don't have it. (There's a sample policy on the *Resources Page*.)

Your Board's Structure: Committees

An executive director and her board chair asked me: What board committees are we required to have? What board committees should we have?

Sound familiar? In my experience, this comes up a lot, particularly for growing nonprofits. Your board's process capacity includes how your board members are organized to do the board's work and effectively work together as they do.

Board problems with committees or task forces are like those related to board meetings, including a lack of focus or purpose, leading to lack of engagement or participation. If there's no mechanism to ensure good follow-through, intended work just won't get done. If a committee is on autopilot, it may have no strategic focus and end up delving into day-to-day operations, getting side-tracked.

These problems can be caused by the same issues as with problematic board meetings: poor agendas, lack of definition of the board's strategic priorities, or failure to provide timely premeeting materials. Some board committees don't have clear charges—what's the result to be achieved? And, like board meetings, maybe there's a lack of committee minutes or a clear written record of actions taken and agreements.

Let's consider Donna's experience. Donna leads a nonprofit that provides space and support for local artists to showcase their work. After serving their community for eight years, they were growing. There were nine board members and no board committees. When I got to know them, they had just completed a planning process, setting strategic goals to diversify their financial base and expand their artistic scope.

With the strategic goals in place, Donna created a first-year operational plan. Initially, the board looked to her and the staff to implement agreed-upon strategies to achieve the strategic goals. The board didn't have a work plan for itself. Joe, the board chair, hadn't led any discussion addressing the board's role in achieving these goals.

Establishing goals for the board and a structure—such as committees—to work on those goals reveals whether the board is organized in the best way possible to get its priority work done. This builds its process capacity.

These board committee problems are caused by board process-capacity issues related to board structure. There could be other underlying issues that I don't dismiss. But if these challenges sound familiar to you, I advise you to start with process capacity and see if putting a good process or policy in place fixes them.

Does your board have the structure in place to efficiently deploy the people resources it has? Is everyone in the right seat? It's not one size fits all. Does your board have unneeded committees or committees working on low priorities? How are you involved with board committees as part of the board's process capacity?

What to Do About It: Create Board Committees Intentionally

Much of your board's work happens in committees and task forces. Board committees should have a specific purpose consistent with governance responsibilities and your strategic goals. Be intentional about them. Form follows function. Know the purpose and then consider board committees to gather the right people to do the board's work.

Remember Donna and her board chair, Joe? The board had no committees or subgroup structure. Once they developed their strategic goals, Donna knew what to do on her end and created an operational plan with her staff. The board simply looked to Donna to act to achieve the goals.

After some coaching, Joe recognized the board had a role in supporting the achievement of the strategic goals, too. He led the board in identifying its appropriate roles in support of each of the goals. This resulted in the board setting annual objectives for itself.

When it came to the "how" of getting the work done, they weren't sure what to do. The lack of board structure—committees—was the problem. It wasn't appropriate for the board as a whole to tackle every objective. And they had ongoing board work to take into consideration. The nine board members worked out who would work on what, and some ongoing committees (such as finance) were established, as were a few strategic ones (such as marketing).

Here are some points to keep in mind and share with your board members:

- To be effective, committee members need to be clear not just about their purpose but also their scope of authority. Do they have any spending authority, for example? Also, it's helpful for everyone to understand the reporting and communication expectations and timelines.
- A board committee should be "charged" in writing—board minutes suffice—stating its purpose and the results the board expects from it. Some call this a committee charter.
- Not every committee member needs to be a member of the board. I'm sure you've heard service on a board committee is a great way to vet a new board member.

Strategically speaking, organizing the work of the board deploys the board's people capacity best. By focusing attention and coordinating board members' efforts, work is accomplished more efficiently. This is done with board meeting agendas and committee structure: board process capacity.

We've covered board process-capacity issues falling within board structure: board meetings and committees. Next, we're going to cover two other vital elements of your board's process capacity: board policies and its systems.

Your Board's Policies

A board policy is a written guideline adopted by the board to chart a course of action. Policies can include the steps that should be taken in certain situations and by whom. In many cases, board policies are where to look for good board practices—leaves in a tree's canopy—the elements of your board's process capacity.

If problems are coming up because the board simply doesn't have a process in place or hasn't discussed the "how" of achieving something, process capacity is the underlying issue, and putting a policy in place may be all you need. There are board policies required by law and others encouraged through regulation—such as by the IRS. If those are lacking, or your board is not complying with them, your board creates an unnecessary risk for your nonprofit and even, in some cases, individual board members.

Bylaws

The scope of bylaws varies widely. I have found some nonprofits think they need to put key board policies in the bylaws. Keep agreements that can be addressed with a policy provision out of your bylaws.

In my experience, including making my own mistakes, nonprofit executives and board members often delay putting needed policies in place until they directly experience the pain of not having them. This is a delicate dance because you don't want to be paranoid, and you can't control everything. And, frankly, having a policy in place won't always safeguard you from board problems.

Reviewing every possible board policy is not within the purpose of this book. But here are examples of five policies impacting you as the executive director and the problems arising when your board doesn't have them.

Conflict of Interest

A conflict of interest occurs when there is a collision between the interests of the organization and an individual's interests—in this case, a board member. One of my clients, Estella, was hiring a new bookkeeper and her board president, Sam, suggested hiring his sister, Elaine, who was an experienced bookkeeper. Sam argued that Elaine would be very committed to the work because of her personal connection to their nonprofit.

On the other hand, Estella was understandably reluctant to supervise the board president's sister. And even though it didn't come up for her, another worry—no matter how unlikely—could be a collusion between Sam and Elaine leading to embezzlement.

While staffing was clearly Estella's decision, Sam's involvement complicated it, and board members didn't have the guidance a policy could provide to back up Estella's concerns.

What to Do About It: Adopt a Conflict-of-Interest Policy

Every board needs a conflict-of-interest policy and agreed-upon procedures for preventing, avoiding, or mitigating conflicts when they occur. Ideally, the policy should include a conflict-of-interest statement, defining conflicts of interest in a board context, the actual policy, and a disclosure form for board members to complete annually. (See samples on the *Resources Page.*) It's worth noting that IRS Form 990 requires you to report about this.

Executive Compensation

Serious problems can occur when determining executive compensation isn't an agreed-upon board process but an ad hoc, quick check-in among board members who want more to support and reward the executive than to make a reasoned, supportable compensation decision. When the board isn't clear, transparent, and consistent about this, the relationship with the executive director may be harmed.

It isn't a popularity contest for sure and, don't laugh, I've seen that. Problems caused by the lack of a good process for determining executive compensation aren't just about IRS compliance.

I got a call from an outraged board member who was new to the board. The board executive committee conducted the executive's evaluation. Their nonprofit had a practice of combining recommendations for the executive's compensation with the evaluation. The board member calling had just learned the only board members who participated in the performance evaluation were the executive committee members. Worse, they were the only ones who *knew* the executive's compensation!

This had apparently been going on for years. New eyes bring new perspectives. The outcome was ultimately positive but keeping everyone working constructively with the executive director on it was a real challenge.

What to Do About It: Develop a Strong Executive Compensation Policy

On your IRS 990 form, you're asked about the process for determining executive compensation and the board's role in it. Documentation of this process as a board policy is essential, and its focus should be on reasonableness. Ideally, your board will create a board task force to oversee the process, but the final review and approval should rest with the full board.

Work with your board to develop an objective practice and policy for this. This should be described in a formal document approved by the board. This helps address any liabilities. Part of the process needs to include the board having accurate information about executive and staff compensation.

No doubt about it, as the executive director, involvement in this could be awkward for you. But your role is to support and inform effective and legally compliant governance practices and policies. Your board will understand. (See a sample on the *Resources Page*.)

Board-Staff Interactions and Grievance Policies

An executive director contacted me to help her deal with a problem I'd seen before: staff going directly to board members with complaints. The complaints in her case were about her. In other cases, I've seen complaints about the nonprofit's operations. The board members felt they needed to hear the employee's complaints and engaged in a lengthy process. They didn't keep the executive informed as they investigated and deliberated about what to do.

The complaints turned out to be unfounded, but the amount of time and lack of information and communication surrounding how the board handled this put severe stress on their relationship with the executive director.

What to Do About It: Create Board-staff Interaction and Grievance Policies

The problem above could have been avoided with a sound staff-board member interaction policy in place, as well as an appropriate grievance procedure in their personnel policies. A staff-board member interaction policy is a tool your board can use when complaints are not directly about the executive director. This policy is valuable in educating board members about what they should do if approached by a staff member. The process should be developed by the full board with your input as the executive director.

If a staff member has a complaint about you as the executive director, even if you have a grievance policy indicating how to handle it, you may not be able to prevent someone from going directly to a board member. Make sure this situation is addressed in board-adopted grievance policies and procedures, and educate your board members about it. Don't forget to include this in your board orientation. A related whistle-blower policy is required in the United States. (See the *Resources Page* for sample policies.)

When You Have Money to Invest

Have you noticed people can be very sensitive or emotional about money? A board I was on had one member who insisted a nonprofit could only have money in insured bank accounts. Another board member argued it was our fiduciary duty to grow our money. He argued on the side of stocks and bonds for a portion of our reserve funds—without taking undue risk.

What did it mean for us? An interesting discussion, but the majority of board members voted to stay out of the stock market. Was it the right decision?

What to Do About It: Develop and Adopt an Investment Policy

If your board oversees a significant reserve or other financial resources, you need a board policy to guide the investment of those resources. Deciding the parameters of risk and expectations for return should be included in it.

Executive and Board Members: Who Can Spend What, When?

One executive director I know was livid when her board chair told her she had no authority to sign a five-hundred-dollar check! I knew colleagues when I was an executive who had experienced something similar. So, when I became CEO of a large nonprofit after two mergers, I asked my board to establish this policy. I didn't want any surprises after authorizing an expenditure. Thankfully, my board was reasonable and didn't tie my hands.

This is important for board members, as well. A nonprofit providing affordable housing in three communities had its offices in an old downtown building they owned. The executive and the board recognized and prioritized in their strategic plan the need to assess the state of the building and develop a plan (and budget) for renovation and repair. They created a board task force to work on this goal.

The executive director, the board chair, and other board members assumed everyone understood board members and board workgroups were not authorized to spend the nonprofit's funds without the board's formal approval. So, it was a big surprise when, during the discussion of the strategic plan goals at a board meeting, the task force chair announced he engaged a structural engineer to assess the building—at the cost of three thousand dollars.

The task force, let alone its chair, wasn't authorized by the board to spend money or sign contracts. In addition to lacking a policy clarifying board members' spending authority, the board hadn't addressed contracting authority. As an executive, you don't want to be presented with a significant reimbursement request you didn't expect from a board member.

What to Do about It: Adopt Executive Spending Authority and Board Member Spending Policies

An executive spending authority policy establishes your decision-making boundaries, as the executive director, for expenditures you can make without the board being involved in the decision. Don't take your spending authority for granted! In my experience, this policy doesn't exist very often. While problems are not very common, damage to the board/executive director relationship can be significant when they do occur.

The board should adopt a policy giving board members crystal clear direction about their spending authority, if any. This policy should also state the board's position on board member expense reimbursement and the process. Beyond the policy, the board may choose to take action when creating a committee or task force "charge" about any spending authority relevant to the group's work. Given that this is about finances and liabilities, you need to be involved in all of this.

The above examples highlight the problems experienced when a board's process capacity doesn't include the board policies it needs to operate effectively and guide good decisions. Having clear board policies makes board operations smoother and more efficient. They're an essential part of your board's process capacity and having them strengthens board performance.

Refer to the *Resources Page* for a list, and some samples, of board policies you want to have.

We've covered board structure and policies—critical components of your board's process capacity. Our tree's canopy is almost full!

Does your board have the consistent practices it needs to be effective? Has your board created systems for its more complex ongoing work—including the work of managing itself? What's missing? Are you reinventing the wheel over and over?

Your Board's Systems

Board responsibilities best addressed by having sound systems in place include board member recruitment, orientation, board self-assessment, and executive director performance evaluation. When defined practices for these are lacking or are not consistent and systematized, it will likely cause numerous problems. As a result, your board's process capacity will be inadequate at best or disastrous at worst. Let's look into problems caused by the lack of consistent, effective practices (or systems) for your board's ongoing work—essential parts of your board's process capacity.

Board Member Recruitment

Gina, an executive director, described for me her board's practices for recruiting new board members:

> *The governance committee was recruiting new board members and, before I was the ED, met without the ED or any staff and did the whole function in a corner somewhere at someone's house. People were approached as if they were doing us a favor. Later, with consultant help, we came at it with the perspective that it's a privilege to serve on our board—they had to be chosen, not just swept off the street.*

Gina and her board members experienced several problems because they lacked a good board recruitment system. Board seats were vacant for a long time as they recreated how to go about finding people. They lacked diversity in many areas, as well as desired expertise. Out of desperation, they recruited people who were not a good fit. Ever heard of a board doing that?

They just didn't have the people they needed to get important board work done. They had a people-capacity problem, but it was caused by a process-capacity issue. Having a strong, effective board requires having the right people in the right seats and a good board member recruitment system to do it.

What to Do About It: Establish an Effective Board Member Recruitment System

The quality of your board is dependent on the people who are on it. We covered in Chapter Two what can happen when your board's people capacity is inadequate—when you either don't have enough people serving, or they're not the right people.

My interviews with executive directors revealed that one of the biggest challenges they have is finding the people they want and need for the board. Experience and research have made it clear that most boards don't have a *system* for recruiting new board members. What they do have is an ad hoc process that gets reinvented from time to time when board members leave the board, leading to this realization: "Oops! We have a vacancy to fill."

I've worked with many executive directors and their boards when they felt desperate to recruit new board members. For example, one was down to three board members, two of which were spouses. Another board had five members who had all been on the board for at least ten years. They weren't just burned out. They were tapped out.

Working with these and others, I discovered the steps we took together were effective regardless of the type of nonprofit, the characteristics of board member candidates they wanted, or other factors. In all these cases, in four to six months, the executive and board members identified, vetted, and elected three to six new board members who met their most desirable strategic criteria and were culturally and otherwise diverse. In addition, they created an ongoing pipeline of desired board member prospects.

The process I coached them through is a consistently effective board member recruitment system, and it has five elements.

Shifting Mindsets

The first is shifting mindsets. Executives confirm with me all the time that the following mindsets—theirs and their board members—are common:

- "People we want don't have time to serve on a board."
- "We've tapped all our networks; there's nowhere else to go."
- "We need people to fundraise, and no one wants to."

Sound familiar?

These mindsets and others like them are barriers to your board member recruitment success. To shift them, you and the board need to have dedicated time together to surface these beliefs, test them by asking what evidence you have they are true, and create agreed-upon statements of *positive* results you intend to achieve. (We'll address mindsets as barriers to diversity, equity, and inclusion in Chapter Six.)

Preparation

The second element of an effective board recruitment system is preparation. You need four things in place before you are ready to recruit:

- Designated board leadership to coordinate the process, such as a governance committee. Remember, you have a crucial role in new board member recruitment and should be part of this group.
- Agreement about expectations of all board members, such as serving on a committee
- Clarity about the board's goals supporting your nonprofit's strategic goals
- Agreement on the criteria you need in new board members, using the strategic goals and related board work as a guide. Recognize you need a board culture of inclusion for any real success diversifying (more in Chapter Six).

A key point: the designated board leadership for recruitment should be *ongoing*. An effective board recruitment system is continuous, not something kicking in only when you have a vacancy. It will ebb and flow depending on your board's needs, but you don't want to miss out on a great new board member—who can serve on a committee if there isn't an open board seat.

Identification

The third element is identification. Once you've prepared, you're ready to go out and find the people you need and want.

There are direct and indirect sources for board member prospects. Direct sources are those people you, board members, staff, and so on, know personally. Indirect sources are people who *could* know the prospects you seek.

Using indirect sources is where I see boards get stuck. They rarely go beyond people they know to identify prospects. To be effective, you're going to have to do that, particularly if you are genuinely committed to diversity. Frankly, it's akin to cold calling. But it works! Ask: who cares about our mission? Who could care? Who knows them?

Brainstorm together with your criteria in mind, make assignments, and have conversations with your identified prospects or those who would know them.

Assessment Process

The fourth element of an effective board member recruitment system is a strong and intentional process for assessing a prospect's fit with your nonprofit and your board. The assessment process should include an in-person meeting and a way for your candidate to experience your mission—perhaps by touring a program.

Don't approach your prospect by "selling" your nonprofit. Your primary job is to get to know the candidate, not the other way around.

Selection and Election

The last elements of an effective board recruitment system are selection and election. If your candidate is still a prospect after the steps above, your leadership group decides whether and when to make the nomination. A vote on the nominee happens at a board meeting.

There are a free training and more information about this proven system on the *Resources Page.* Your board's process capacity isn't complete if it doesn't include a structured, repeatable, consistent system for board member recruitment.

Board Member Orientation

When I was an executive director, we had a board orientation, but it lacked key things. It did a great job educating board members about our nonprofit, but it didn't include much about being a nonprofit board member. Without covering governing roles and responsibilities, board members at best don't know what they don't know and, at worse, think their job includes aspects of your job.

Unfortunately, this is not rare. My research with over a hundred board members found 75 percent had *never* had a formal orientation to their governing roles and responsibilities. Incredible! And some had over twenty years of nonprofit board service. By the way, a board manual can be a great tool, but it's no substitute for a well-prepared orientation.

If your board orientation is inconsistent from board member to board member, your board members' understanding of their roles versus yours, as the executive director, will be inconsistent, too. I've seen this cause micromanagement, interference with staff work, and inappropriate communication with external community stakeholders.

I'm sure you've heard about board members who get on the board and then hold back while they figure things out. I remember a conversation I had with someone who had been on the board of a local museum for almost a year. He'd never served on a nonprofit board before and was learning how the board functioned. He didn't feel comfortable yet in his role.

He confessed he rarely spoke up at the meetings even though he was usually a vocal financial services executive. He didn't fully understand what it meant to be a board member. The result was a true waste of his time and a real loss for the museum of any resources or benefits he might have been able to bring.

Unless your board orientation program *fully* informs board members about what governing does and *can* include, your new board members aren't going to hit the ground running, which is a huge waste.

What to Do About It: Develop a Complete Board Member Orientation System

The most significant opportunity you have to ensure your board members realize their full potential to advance your mission is to orient them effectively. To optimize its process capacity, your board needs a comprehensive and consistent board orientation system.

An effective board member orientation system has two components: orientation to your nonprofit and to nonprofit governance—what it means to be a board member. Here are three tips to help you have a *complete* board orientation with a strong governance component:

Start with Why

Start with why. Board members need to know why the job of being a board member is essential. Share some specific examples of how your nonprofit has benefited from the results your board has created.

Explain the Board's Place in the Organization

Inform board members how the board fits within your organizational structure. Help them understand their roles and responsibilities *as distinct from yours and other staff.*

Present the Opportunities

Broaden the scope of the information to include the *opportunities* board members have, to have fun and do interesting things—such as building relationships with stakeholders, framing your messaging, advocating and being an ambassador of the mission, team building for the board, and creating a strong partnership with you.

There's a free training and more information about a comprehensive and effective board orientation system on the *Resources Page*. It also includes how you can have a system without taking a lot of your time. Board orientation is a critical component of your board's process capacity.

Board Self-assessment

Without occasionally answering the question, "How are we doing?" boards can drift off course. Board members may know in theory their roles and responsibilities, but what about in practice?

Your board members may be unaware of good governing practices because they haven't assessed themselves against any standards of performance. Or they've used a quick just-grab-this-survey-off-the-internet process that yields meaningless results.

Without a good board self-assessment process, you're missing out on leverage you could have to suggest improvements in your board's functioning. Also, lack of insight about how effective boards work keeps your board's potential untapped, with numerous implications for your mission and you.

What to Do About It: Establish an Evidence-based Board Self-assessment System

A good board self-assessment process is one of the most critical elements of your board's process capacity. We now have research showing the very fact of conducting a self-assessment improves board performance. If you want to have a board that's truly an asset and you know changes are needed, then start with a board assessment. A board assessment demonstrates that the board values accountability and is modeling it for your whole nonprofit.

A quality board self-assessment requires time and attention from the board. The results should drive a plan for board improvement. For this reason, I recommend boards do self-assessments every couple of years. Unless you have a considerable turnover or significant change on your board, chances are things aren't going to change so fast to warrant an annual board self-assessment.

An effective board assessment includes these five steps:

1. Determine which board committee will own and shepherd the process.

2. Design the process addressing some key questions:

   a) Determine who will be involved, and how. As the executive director, how is your input going to be included (it should be!)?

   b) Identify what criteria or standards will be used to assess the board (Seek out an evidence-based tool.)

   c) Consider how the data will be collected. Survey? Interviews? Focus group?

3. Gather and analyze the data (This step can undermine your entire process unless the people analyzing and interpreting the data are respected as objective by the other board members and understand validity and reliability concepts.)

4. Communicate and discuss the findings.

5. Create an action plan for improvement.

You owe it to your mission to have the best possible board. Evaluating how you're doing and committing to needed improvements will get you there. An effective board assessment requires a quality process using a valid methodology. There's more information about how to get help on the *Resources Page*.

Board self-assessment, when done right, is an important component of your board's process capacity.

The Executive Director Performance Evaluation

Effective leadership requires clarity of expectations and feedback on an ongoing basis. But many executive directors don't get evaluated. Do you? You may not mind if the board fails to do your performance evaluation, but you should. It's one of the board's most important governing responsibilities.

It's not uncommon for a board's process for the executive director evaluation to be inconsistent from year to year or invalid in its methodology, resulting in less than meaningful feedback for everyone involved, especially you. And a flawed process can create tension between you and your board.

Anaya was an experienced and well-respected executive director of a hospice and in-home support services nonprofit. She had been the executive director for almost twenty years. I had been privileged to work with her and her board many times. I observed a very collaborative and strategic relationship.

So, I was quite surprised when Anaya called me, obviously upset. The board had completed her performance evaluation, and the results were less than the typical glowing report she was used to. We met, and I reviewed the final report and the instrument the board used to survey each of the board members.

I found the instrument had a poor rating scale despite the fact it was produced by a very reputable national organization. For example, here were the rating options:

- ❑ Exceeds expectations
- ❑ Meets expectations
- ❑ Fails to meet expectations.

Really? How could an executive be confident each board member was defining the expectations the same way, let alone what "exceeds" or "fails to meet" them meant?

With further discussion and some training, the board adopted a different approach, and it all worked out quite well for Anaya—and the board members. I don't mean to imply all executive director evaluations should be glowing, or a long-tenured executive can't be ineffective. In this case, Anaya was very open to constructive feedback, but the flawed process didn't communicate at all what the board intended.

Too much is at stake for this critical part of your board's process capacity to not be done with a thoughtful, appropriate practice—one that can be relied on for useful and valid results.

What to Do about It: Develop an Executive Director Performance Evaluation System

It's most effective when this system is created jointly by you and your board. It's complex and requires thoughtfulness. A quick approach isn't worth doing, and you deserve better. Designing your evaluation system's elements involves answering some key questions—while considering your nonprofit's unique context and priorities. One size does not fit all!

Your full board is responsible for the process. It should address the following questions and steps:

- Who leads the process?
- Who's involved and how? (It can include board members, direct reports, other staff, key stakeholders, an outside consultant, and so on.) It depends on your nonprofit.

The board should gather information from the staff you directly supervise as part of your evaluation while ensuring the process doesn't deteriorate into a popularity contest.

- What data will be collected? There are two types of data to collect:

    - Performance data: items relevant to the position, such as progress on strategic priorities and financial and organizational performance; and

    - Professional development data: the executive's strengths and areas for improvement.

- How is the data collected? As you make these choices, consider who is involved and their comfort and skill levels. Performance data often comes from organizational reports. Collecting data about strengths and areas for improvement usually involves a survey or interviews, or both. Avoid inappropriate or ineffective rating scales.

- Analyzing the data. A common pitfall is board members over-reacting to outlier comments. Unless it's something illegal or unethical (which the board needs to investigate), one or two complaints among many should be ignored. Trust me on this. I'm a researcher. How board members analyze and interpret the data collected is critical.

- Delivering the results. A board subgroup should discuss the initial results with the executive director and allow the executive to provide a written statement in response.

- Lastly, a final written report is discussed among the full board in an executive session, and a copy is later given to the executive.

I've included on the *Resources Page* a description of an executive director performance evaluation system assessed and commended as one of the best they'd seen by a national accreditation organization.

Having good and complete board practices (systems) for board member recruitment, orientation, board self-assessment, and the executive director's performance evaluation are essential elements of your board's process capacity.

There are other board responsibility areas: good board practices enhance planning, mission performance evaluation, fundraising, communication, advocacy, and financial oversight. They are all part of your board's process capacity, too.

In this chapter, we covered board problems rooted in the board's process capacity: its structure, policies, and practices or systems.

Key Lessons

- Follow the tips for productive board meetings.
- Adopt a consent agenda.
- Create board committees intentionally and use them effectively.
- Coach the board chair as needed in effective facilitation.
- Develop and adopt the board policies you need.
- Establish an ongoing, effective board member recruitment system.
- Put a complete board orientation in place.
- Assess the board.
- Develop an objective executive director performance evaluation.

Wrapping It Up

Problems with your board may be caused by a lack of board people or process capacity. Your board's people capacity consists of the board members and non-board volunteers, including their skills, talents, and knowledge. It includes you as the executive director. And board process capacity includes its structure, policies, and practices or systems.

There's a *lot* within this capacity dimension. This is usually the first and sometimes the only place nonprofit leaders address a problem or performance failure with their boards. Putting the right people on the bus, orienting them well, having a good structure to get work done, and having sound systems and policies in place for board operations, may be enough.

When everything else is working well, unleashing more value from the board may just be a matter of addressing issues of capacity. Board value is untapped, though, when "if only" thinking, reflected in the following comments, masks a deeper underlying cause:

- "If the board would just get clear on our roles and responsibilities . . ."
- "Once we get more people on the board . . ."
- "We just need to figure out what committees we need . . ."

Are your assessments of what you need accurate? It's easier to change board activities and structure than individuals and their behavior! Considering only board capacity can cause you to miss issues you need to address.

If you have a board problem you think can be addressed within this capacity dimension, like feeding, growing, and adding leaves to a tree's canopy, review what to do from this chapter and Chapter Two, and check out the *Resources Page*.

If you know, or just sense, there is more to what you and your board are struggling with, then I'm confident you'll find an answer in the upcoming chapters on connection and culture. Go deeper!

CHAPTER FOUR

Connection: People

The message came to me from Jessica at 7 p.m. "Hi Mary," she wrote. "I'm reaching out to you via LinkedIn because I don't want to use my work email. Something happened today, and I feel very frustrated and hurt. But I'm not sure there's anything I can do about it." Jessica was one of my executive coaching clients. We arranged a time to talk ASAP.

She was in her fourth year as the executive director of a nonprofit hospital foundation established six years before to raise money to fund special health-promoting programs in their moderately sized community. The foundation's mission was limited to funding programs operated by the hospital.

Jessica had successfully increased the funds raised year over year during her tenure—even though the board she inherited was the proverbial "not a fundraising" board. I knew Jessica's relationship with her board chair, Frank, had been strained.

Frank was a founding board member who, despite continuous assurances for Jessica that he and the other board members thought highly of her, frequently undermined, and even usurped, her authority.

Here are a couple of examples.

The relationship between Jessica as the foundation executive and the CEO of the hospital they supported was a critical one for both organizations. Jessica met monthly with the CEO to share updates about the funding received for hospital programs.

If a board member has a special connection with a key influencer, that can be an asset. But the executive director and board members must be able to trust that important information will be shared quickly. The hospital CEO and Frank did not have a special connection. There was no organizational reason they would meet.

When Jessica and I spoke, she told me that Frank had met with the CEO without her and discussed with him a well-liked, important, and foundation-funded program. The CEO informed Frank (but not Jessica) of the hospital's decision to eliminate the program. This decision had significant implications for the foundation.

Frank not only didn't call or attempt to connect directly with Jessica after the meeting but, bypassing her, emailed a report of the meeting to the full board. The failure to include or reference Jessica in the communication didn't go unnoticed by other board members. A few of them contacted Jessica and expressed their own frustration with her being bypassed. But, they weren't willing to say anything to Frank about it even though they acknowledged he had undermined Jessica's authority by meeting on his own with the hospital CEO.

This wasn't the first time Frank had done something like this. On another occasion, Frank obtained an updated copy of the foundation's MOU with the hospital (which Jessica did not have or know about) and discussed changes he thought should be made directly with the hospital CEO. The first Jessica heard of it was at the board meeting at which Frank presented it for discussion.

This exemplifies the kinds of connection challenges I repeatedly hear about between executive directors and their board chairs and among the board members and executives. Problems with board connections and what to do about them are what we're covering in this chapter.

These connections are like the tree branches drawing together the nourishment from the leaves—as board connections draw together your board's capacity. Weak and flimsy branches won't do the job!

Connection: People and Process

Boards and executives often look to structure, role clarification, and rules to improve functioning or solve issues. When you do, applying the strategies you learned in the last two chapters can work. But if problems persist, personalities and relationship dynamics may underlie the issues. Then, interventions focused on capacity won't have a lasting impact and may have no impact at all. Strategies targeting person-to-person connections must come into play.

The discussion of your board's connection processes—how your board develops as an effective team—is in the next chapter. Here, we're focusing on the people dynamics—your board's people connections.

We often hear the phrase, "It's all about relationships." Well, it is. The quality and scope of relationships among board members and between the board members and the executive director make a huge difference for your nonprofit organization. So much about boards can be enhanced by focusing on interpersonal connections. The quality of those connections depends on the relationship-building competence and interpersonal dynamics of board members as individuals and as a group.

The scope of connections relevant to your nonprofit and you as its leader is broad. While external connections are critical to your nonprofit's success, our focus here is on the board members' connections with you and with each other. But rest assured, the principles and strategies you'll learn here apply to all the connections you have.

Problems with your board's people connections fall into two primary categories: your relationship with your board chair and your relationship with the board and board members. I've also included a third section giving you some additional tips for when things go wrong.

Your Board's People Connections

In the last chapters, we covered why and how to have the right people on your board. But having the right people on your board hardly matters if you don't have trusting relationships with them. All the benefits from the gifts someone brings to the board will be unrealized if you're not in relationships with each other in a meaningful way.

Too often, we take it for granted people know how to build and nurture relationships—big mistake! Not everyone is able or willing to build strong interpersonal relationships. Unfortunately, we all know people who dismiss the importance of connection, are insecure and self-focused, and can actually do more harm than good. The strength or lack of board members' interpersonal skills will play out among board members and with you as executive director. Your board's effectiveness is greatly influenced by these critical connections.

Let's start with your connection with your board chair. I'll touch on some of the problems commonly experienced. Then we'll delve into several strategies to build that relationship—some unique to your connection with your board chair and some which apply to your relations with individual board members too.

The Board Chair/Executive Director Relationship

My research and that of others reinforce the understanding that the board chair/executive director relationship's quality is critical for a nonprofit's success and stability. For example, in nonprofits of all sizes, the executive's tenure is impacted by the degree of perceived board support. About 30 percent of executive directors cite weak, or outright lack of, board support as the reason they resign. The board chair is the focal point of that support. (See the reports available on the *Resources Page.*)

You know firsthand as an executive director the challenges inherent in board chairs rotating year after year, let alone the challenges of working with someone who is not a good fit or supportive collaborator. Every time you have a new board chair, you start over building the connection. Each of these relationships is unique.

You may not have insight into why your board chair behaves a particular way. You're likely just trying to cope with it when it's challenging. A coping strategy I've seen, rooted in anticipation of board chair turnover, is executive directors who hunker down and wait it out. Remember Claudia, the new executive director of a housing nonprofit in Chapter One? Her board chair didn't believe the board needed to conduct a self-assessment, so Claudia decided to wait until his term was up and see if the new board chair was receptive. Turns out he was, but what was the cost of the wait?

When this happens, sometimes more than just a board self-assessment is put on hold. I've seen strategic initiatives critical to the mission put off as well. I acknowledge sometimes there won't be anything else you can do. This just underscores the importance of this relationship. And, like so many other relationships, being proactive to make it wonderful can make a huge difference.

You may be blessed with a great relationship with your board chair and a great board chair. By nature, I'm optimistic and quick to see the bright side, so it's a bit out of character for me to point out there are no guarantees things won't change. I encourage those of you who love your board chairs to keep reading. Some of the tips I offer in this section will help you with a future challenging relationship.

Unfortunately, not-so-uncommon problems with a board chair/executive director relationship include micromanagement, absenteeism, power struggle, and being patronized. Here are a few examples I've seen.

Micromanagement

Our City Services for Youth was a nonprofit over twenty-five years old with proven effectiveness in achieving targeted outcomes for high-risk youth. The board chair had worked as a youth counselor for many years. She was passionate about the mission—what attracted her to board service.

But once she became the board chair, it became clear she had strong views about effective strategies for working with youth. As a result, she frequently would grill and sometimes challenge the executive director about programmatic approaches. She clearly lacked trust in his judgment, and, as a result, he avoided meeting with her and held back on information.

She not only challenged him when they met one-on-one but questioned him at board meetings. The tension between them caused discomfort among the board members. Her critical comments had the effect of eroding the confidence other board members had in the executive director. As a result, they could not align around strategic priorities, and essential work supporting the mission stagnated.

Patronized

I've known some executives who felt patronized by their board chairs. In more than one instance, these board chairs were corporate executives with minimal nonprofit experience. They saw most nonprofits, especially small ones, as inferior organizations to businesses.

One board chair, Carol, worked in a famous technology company in Silicon Valley. The executive director, Laura, had been in her position for just eight months but was a mature leader. Laura told me, "Carol treats me like a glorified manager" and "refers to herself as my boss." Carol sets the board agenda on her own and "allows" Laura a "piece" of it.

Laura tried to discuss this directly with Carol, who would seem to "get it" but then fall back into the same patronizing pattern. When I last heard from Laura, she was seriously considering resigning.

Absenteeism

Rafael, another executive director, called for advice. His nonprofit was experiencing severe financial problems when a key government contract wasn't renewed. Rafael wanted and needed his board president, Ralph, as a sounding board to help vet how to present this challenge to the board and how much information to share. When Ralph was available, Rafael found him to be a great thought partner. Unfortunately, Ralph was away on business travel most of the time. Rafael tried engaging with a couple of other board members, but they were reluctant to offer advice for fear Ralph would feel they were circumventing him. As a result, Rafael was missing a valuable source of support.

Power Struggles

When I started coaching Ethan, executive director of an art gallery with educational programs for youth, I saw a power struggle firsthand. The board chair, Ben, had stepped into an interim executive director role after the prior executive had retired. When Ethan was hired, Ben was unable to release the authority he had as the interim executive.

This manifested in a variety of ways, but here's one example. Ben chaired the board fund development committee. After Ethan had been in his position for several months, Ben simply bypassed him, contacted all the development staff, and invited them to attend a training with him—without consulting Ethan. When Ethan raised this issue with Ben, Ben dismissed Ethan's concerns and said that, as board chair, it was appropriate for him to contact staff directly anytime.

Divergent Priorities

Another board chair/executive director connection problem is disagreement on how to approach important work. As we covered, having agreed-upon strategic goals is critical for your nonprofit's and your board's functioning. Problems arise when there is disagreement on the strategies needed to achieve those goals.

The board chair leads your board's important work supporting the achievement of the strategic goals. As executive director, you lead the day-to-day operations to achieve those goals. These two paths of activity need to be aligned to achieve results. The board chair's leadership role with the board influences this alignment.

I've seen this lack of alignment cause a rift in the board chair/executive relationship. At a board retreat I facilitated, the board and executive agreed a new staff position was needed to achieve a programmatic goal they had adopted in their strategic plan. While developing its own work plan to support the newly updated strategic plan goals, the board set an annual fundraising objective to fund half the position.

To keep the focus on strategic goals, it had been the board's practice to have its work plan objectives on each board meeting agenda—not to report every meeting but to keep the board focused. The board chair and the executive typically worked out the board meeting agenda together.

This time, though, after the retreat, the board chair consistently emphasized all the board was working on *except* fundraising. He kept telling the executive he trusted the development committee's chair to handle the board's fundraising objective and didn't see a need to call attention to it at the meetings.

Despite concerns raised by the executive about the lack of board progress on its objective, the chair continued to discount the fundraising work's importance and focused the board on other things. The relationship eroded significantly as a result. The executive stopped consulting with the chair and avoided meetings with him other than about the board meeting agenda.

Authority, Roles, and Boundaries

Micromanagement, being patronized, or experiencing power struggles can arise from a lack of understanding of the appropriate authority, roles, and boundaries inherent in the executive director and board chair positions. You may be able to address the problem with education as a board capacity issue. But in some cases, it isn't enough for a board chair to get information telling him the parameters of his role; his personality and needs may trump that understanding.

I've heard of board chairs several times who think their roles and authority include their being the executive director's supervisor. Despite knowledge to the contrary, I've seen them continue to act as if they were. In Jessica and Frank's story, you can see Frank overstepped the boundaries of his role several times. Thinking about authority, roles, and boundaries can help you assess what's underlying a problem you have with your board chair.

This critical, interdependent board chair/executive director connection falls along a continuum from very dysfunctional to exciting and enriching. The most critical factor to make it the best it can be is trust. Next, we'll get into what trust is and how you can build it.

Armed with evidence-based knowledge, you'll have the tools and strategies to establish and strengthen your connections with your board chair. And you can apply all you're going to learn here to your relationship with the board, including each board member.

What to Do about It: Know What Trust Is and Practice Diverse Interactions to Build It

I think it's safe to say whatever's been written about the board chair/executive director connection (and the board/ executive relationship) calls out the importance of trust. "Mutual trust" is a mantra for what is needed to build and sustain a positive leadership collaboration at the top of nonprofit organizations. This collaboration has a profound influence on a nonprofit's results.

My research with paired executive directors and board chairs reveals a lot about what goes on in those relationships and the characteristics of those with a very positive impact on their nonprofits. Productivity, board engagement, staff morale, reputation, resources, community engagement, and a host of other important organizational performance indicators are influenced by the quality of the executive/board chair connection. And the quality of the connection is dependent on the level of trust. (There's an article about this on the *Resources Page.*)

When asked to define trust, people usually describe behaviors—not trust itself. Trust is a feeling, not a behavior. When you trust someone, you *feel* confident the person has your interests at heart, best case, or at least will not harm you, worst case.

Trust is not purely an on-or-off phenomenon. Yes, you either trust someone, or you don't. But, levels of trust range from high to low. When you do trust someone, it's how *much* you trust the person that influences the relationship. Unfortunately, building trust is easier said than done, and many people simply don't know how or leave it to chance.

The strength of your connection develops as a result of the one-on-one interactions you have. The first step in learning how to build trust is to know there are five types of interpersonal interactions executives and board members can have. Let's learn what those are.

Fact-sharing

Fact-sharing is a one-way giving of information. It doesn't involve engaging the other person in the exchange. Fact-sharing is the most basic of interpersonal interactions.

Idea-sharing

The idea-sharing interaction type is characterized by brainstorming, problem-solving, or thinking things through together. In contrast to fact-sharing, idea-sharing involves both parties' engagement in the interaction—a two-way exchange. The focus of board chair/executive idea-sharing ranges from a quick check-in to consulting each other about organizational issues or the board chair serving as a sounding board for the executive.

Knowledge-sharing

Knowledge-sharing is a learning or coaching type of interaction. This type is distinct from sharing facts or ideas in that there is a teaching component and identifiable content learned as a result. It could be about the organization, something outside the organization, or about the person. The most common examples of knowledge-sharing are coaching the executive by the board chair and the executive teaching the board chair about the organization or nonprofits.

Feelings-sharing

Executive and board chair descriptions of expressed support, reassurance, caring, or appreciation are characteristic of a feelings-sharing type of interaction.

Give-and-Take Interpersonal Interaction

When you or your board chair adapt to the other's style, personality, or preferences, you're engaging in the give-and-take type of interpersonal interaction. It also includes working out differences. The give-and-take dynamic includes, but goes beyond, the executive adapting to a new board chair. It occurs in strong board chair/executive relationships when both make changes to align with or accommodate each other.

The more diverse your types of interactions with your board chair are, the stronger the level of trust in your relationship will be. The amount of time you spend together isn't what really matters—the *quality* of the time is.

What to Do about It: Build Trust to the Identification-based Trust Level

I created a model for trust-building in the workplace with nonprofits in mind. The core of the model is three cumulative levels of trust. Understanding these levels and their cumulative quality will help you know how to build trust with your board chair (and your board members, too). Here they are.

Calculus-based Trust

The first and lowest level of trust I call calculus-based trust. It's the result of making a quick calculation of the pros and cons of trusting someone. Calculus-based trust comes from you choosing (mostly unconsciously) to act from trust even when you don't know the person at all.

For example, you're starting a new job, and you trust the bookkeeper, whom you don't know, will get your paycheck out on time. Or you get on the road and trust the people driving on the other side aren't going to come over the line and collide with you! You don't know them, but you trust them at this very basic level.

Knowledge-based Trust

The next level of trust, knowledge-based trust, is of moderate strength and more complex than calculus-based trust. It's the trust we can build as we get to know each other. This is the level of trust we're most familiar with and associate most often with the relationships we have.

There are three subtypes of knowledge-based trust exemplified when you consistently tell the truth (communication subtype), meet your commitments (contractual subtype), or demonstrate you're competent (competence subtype). Many behaviors build trust within this level—some you may not have thought of.

For example, when you give feedback to or train one of your staff, you're building trust by conveying, perhaps subtlety or subconsciously, you believe the person is worthy of your time and can learn and grow. When you openly receive feedback from others, you're building trust by being vulnerable—open to their judgments—and by conveying to them that their experience of you matters.

Identification-based Trust

This brings us to the third and highest level of trust—which is not what you might expect among leaders "on the job." At this level, you don't just know each other; you *identify* with each other. This is identification-based trust. Your understanding of each other is much more personal—you have opened up and developed a personal bond rooted in shared experiences or interests.

One critical obstacle to building high levels of trust is the belief our workplace relationships, especially at the top, must be characterized by boundaries around our personal lives. We must be "professional." While being professional is good, building a high level of trust at work requires our relationships to be appropriately personal.

The executives and board chairs I interviewed who had this level of trust said:

- "We can finish each other's sentences."
- "I know she would do what I would do in that situation."
- "He can speak for me when I'm not there to be the spokesperson, and we get great leverage of our time and leadership as a result."

To get to the level of identification-based trust, you must get personal. Appropriately personal, of course! But personal, nonetheless. Not everyone is comfortable with this, and some personalities won't mix well. But the benefits of a strong relationship "at the top" for your nonprofit are huge.

What did board chairs and executives do to build identification-based trust? These leaders came to identify with each other by sharing meals together, meeting and getting to know each other's families, talking about what was going on in their personal lives, learning about common interests and sharing them in some way, and proactively supporting each other's success.

Little things, like sharing family pictures, knowing about and following each other's children's hobbies or sports activities, asking questions, telling stories, learning personal connections to the mission, giving small unexpected gifts or greeting cards, connecting on your common ground—these are all ways you can develop high trust with your board chair.

One executive director told me her board chair knew she collected teddy bears. For no particular reason, he gave her a teddy bear. She proudly and affectionately showed it to me. She kept it right on her desk. This was just one example of how they were "getting personal." This may sound hokey, silly, or sentimental to you, but this pair accomplished changes in state legislation and moved the organization farther in their two years together than had been done before in many more. I found the strongest executive/board chair relationships with the most positive organizational impact had identification-based trust.

Striving to have identification-based trust with your board chair and individual board members is worth the time and effort.

My research indicates, when you do, the energy and synergy in your relationship will spread throughout your nonprofit, productivity will improve, staff morale will grow, board members will be more engaged, and board relationships will be stronger and leveraged externally in new ways.

What to do: Build Your Connection with Your Board Chair

In addition to building trust, the following two key strategies will get your connection with your board chair off to a great start and building:

Meet One-on-One

Meet one-on-one early in the relationship—even before your board chair steps into the role, if possible. In this first meeting, start by listening and ask: What does success look like in this role for your board chair? What are your board chair's motivations for being in this role? (Hopefully, it wasn't just by default.) What will make your relationship with each other a success?

Next, it's your turn to share the same. Discuss how you will measure success and identify the indicators to watch for. This will help you go even deeper together about your expectations and hopes.)

This first meeting and subsequent ones are the time to learn each other's preferences, including being tactically versus strategically oriented, detail-oriented versus big picture, focused on process versus outcomes, introverted versus extroverted, fast versus slow to make decisions, and so on.

In this first meeting, review, discuss, and agree on the key priorities for your nonprofit and for the board. What are each of your priority goals for the twelve months you'll be working together? What do you need or expect from each other to accomplish those?

Finally, explore together the professional development opportunities you would each like to have over the coming year. You may have covered this in your performance evaluation with the full board but, even so, it's helpful to remind the board chair.

How Often Will You Connect?

In your first meeting, agree on how and how often you will connect with each other. I recommend you check in at least every other week in a telephone conversation. Allow a half-hour for this call. In addition, commit to an in-person meeting—coffee, lunch—monthly. Sharing a meal together can build trust.

Since you've already shared your goals with each other, these monthly contacts are when you report progress, discuss challenges, and cover anything else the two of you need to share, given you comprise the top leadership of your nonprofit. This is when you formulate the board agenda together—an opportunity for you to keep things focused on strategic and mission issues, avoiding the day-to-day.

The Board/Executive Director Relationship

Because we're talking about people and interpersonal dynamics, it should be no surprise the problems with the *board*/executive director relationship, and even *board member*/ executive relationships, are much the same as those we've just covered in the *board chair*/executive relationship.

Micromanagement

Perhaps the most common board/executive director relationship problem is micromanagement. If this happens because your board doesn't understand its roles and responsibilities, it's a board capacity problem. But it's a board connection problem when it's rooted in a lack of trust.

The board members may know they shouldn't meddle in day-to-day operations. Still, when board members don't trust the executive director enough, they will often delve into operations inappropriately for reassurance. They feel responsible.

You may experience micromanagement when a board member chairs a committee. This can come up when board members feel they are more experienced, knowledgeable, etc., than you in a specific management area. Whether it's fundraising, financial management, HR practices, or others, the board member with expertise may overstep boundaries and start telling you how to do your job.

Whether in the boardroom or outside of it, you may also have a problem with a board member who simply disagrees with your recommendations, strategic goals, or something else you're working on. Some people just can't let go, and this can show up at a meeting or when a board member is interacting with you, perhaps trying to get you to revisit the issue or just taking up your time over and over again rehashing things. Depending on the attitude of the board member, you may also experience the situation as patronizing.

Micromanagement can also be a sign of board members who need to control or have big egos. It's not often one board member's ego, control, or other personal style or personality issue influences the entire board's relationship with the executive director. However, these board members may dominate the board and cause all kinds of problems with the board/executive relationship—including those discussed below.

Authority, Roles, and Boundaries

For a group of leaders to work effectively together, they *all* need to understand and agree on the roles, authority, and boundaries they have relative to each other. This is true for you and the board, together, as the leadership team for your nonprofit.

Again, I'm not just talking about a misunderstanding about roles that can be clarified through training. In this case, board members may know their roles, but the interpersonal dynamics are influenced by them not respecting your authority. An example comes to mind.

Kobe was a brand-new executive director of a children's day school and childcare center. He had never been an executive director before. The school was faith-based and had been founded by a group of nuns. The nuns had worked with the prior executive for quite a while and, frankly, let her runs things.

But, with Kobe, they were unable to establish a relationship fully honoring his role. He asked me to help by conducting board training on roles and responsibilities—a common strategy for this type of problem, as I've noted. But, when the underlying issue is rooted in the relationship, it won't help much.

Kobe and the nuns on the board—a majority of board members, by the way—had not invested in building their relationship. They focused on the work of the school and center and were neither proactive nor intentional about how they were working together. The board members saw Kobe as inexperienced and would not relinquish authority to him for spending, for example, or engage him as a leadership partner in board development.

When I was conducting the workshop with them, and the content dealt with board member recruitment, I was flabbergasted to learn Kobe was not only not involved in meeting with new board member prospects but was kept utterly in the dark about them until the board elected them. When I asked about this, the board members informed me it was a conflict of interest for Kobe to be involved. They wouldn't budge on this point.

When you have an interpersonal problem with a board member, the main difference from issues like Kobe experienced is individual board members don't have the same level of sanctioned authority. In the case of committee chairs, there is authority, but it's not comparable to that of the board chair or the board as a whole.

There are times when, without sanctioned authority, a board member has undue influence over other board members. An individual board member may also, in effect, usurp the authority and role of the board chair—especially if the board chair is a weak leader. Because of this, dealing with that board member can be just like dealing with a challenging board chair for you.

Another problem with roles and boundaries you may experience with a board member or two is bypassing you and going to staff to express opinions or, worse, give directions. As with many of these examples, if it's merely a matter of educating the board member about roles, authority, and boundaries, it's a people-capacity issue you now know how to fix. But when board members are reluctant or unable to relinquish inappropriate behavior, it's likely a connection problem and creates havoc in your relationship.

The Delicate Dance

Problems with the connection between you and the board can arise when, as a group, the board is unable to effectively manage the natural tension between supporting your success and supervising your performance. This seeming contradiction in roles between objectively checking up on you and being a supportive champion can create a paradox in the relationship difficult to manage and balance.

You're not only supervised by a *group*—where else does this happen!?—you look to them to include you as a member. After all, you're leading together to advance your nonprofit's mission. This, of course, contributes to the complexity of the connection dynamics. I mention it here because you may experience the board moving in and out of these roles: one moment supporting and cheering you forward and another stepping back and scrutinizing you. Problems occur in your relationship when you need, want, and expect one, and they are delivering the other.

Problematic Board Processes

In Chapter Three, we covered the importance of effective board processes, not the least of which are board member recruitment, the executive director performance evaluation, and even how executive sessions are handled. Having effective processes in place will prevent board/executive connection problems. But if those processes are poor or poorly executed, damage to the relationship can occur—the story in Chapter Three of Anaya's experience with her evaluation is an example.

When connections are damaged, putting a new or better process in place won't be enough. Whoever's involved needs to rebuild trust and repair other aspects of the relationship as well as address the board's process capacity issue. You can look at the trust-building action steps above and what to do below for strategies.

What to Do about It: Start with Why

Building a strong connection with your board and board members, and your board chair, too, begins with your motivation. Are you motivated to invest the time and energy it takes? So often, we work *in* relationships, but we don't think to work *on* them. It requires you to do two things: be proactive and intentional. To do both effectively, you need to know your personal *why*.

Why do these relationships with the board chair, board members, and the board matter? In the workplace, the quality of any relationship can facilitate information sharing, promote innovation and new ideas, reduce the time it takes to get something done, and build influence. There are personal benefits, too, such as reduced stress and increased life satisfaction.

I strongly encourage you not to take this for granted. Spend some time thinking about and listing out your reasons for building these critical connections. Exploring your why at a deep level will boost your motivation to invest in them.

What to Do about It: Build Your Connection with Your Board and Board Members

In addition to building trust using the strategies discussed above, you can strengthen your connections with your board by understanding and acting on the four factors we know to influence this vital relationship. Those are executive assets (your resources for influence), alignment (in sync on mission and strategy), communication (what, when, and how), and managing roles and expectations. (Golensky, M. (1993). *Nonprofit Management & Leadership, 4(2)*, 177-191.)

Many of the actions you can take within these four factors are trust-building behaviors, but these give you a different perspective about what to do to strengthen your connection. These four factors will also help you with your future board chair. Typically, chairs have been serving on your board before being elected. You'll have a head start on your connection with your future chair if you're intentional about addressing these four factors with the full board.

Whenever you can, seek opportunities to address these factors with the board and give board members opportunities to do the same with you.

Executive Assets

What are your resources for influence? These are the foundation for building competence trust with your board. You need to know your strengths and the more tangible assets you bring to the executive director position.

What are executive assets? Perhaps the most basic include whether you hold the position full-time or part-time and your tenure—how long you have been an executive director—with your current nonprofit or another? Do you have any specific professional status, such as a license or credential? What is your education? Are you bilingual? How extensive is your relevant experience, and what expertise can you claim?

Something you may not have thought of as an asset is your interpersonal network. Well-networked executives often can solve problems more quickly, have resources for better decision-making, and leverage their connections to enhance goal achievement. As a result of your network, memberships you hold, or other connections, you likely have more efficient access to information than you would otherwise.

No doubt you highlighted these assets with the board when you were being considered for the position. You shared them via your resume, references, and in interviews. Maybe it was recently, but what if it wasn't? And, what if there are new board members since you were hired?

I know very few executives who even think to share the same level of information about themselves with new board members they shared with the board selection committee. And if you've been the executive for a while, you probably haven't updated information with your board at a level you would if you were being hired all over again. Your assets have grown, if only by virtue of being on the job! Don't hide this light under a bushel too long.

Of course, you don't want to brag but look for opportunities (*at least* at the time of your performance evaluation) to provide an update for board members of how you've grown your executive assets—how you have developed professionally.

The more executive assets you have and your board members know about, the greater your perceived competence will be. As a result, your board will have a higher level of trust in you. The same is true for your knowledge about board members, so seek ways to learn as much as you can.

Alignment

Another factor influencing your relationship with board members is how aligned you are with them. You discover this—and so do they—by how you experience agreement with each other in at least four areas: mission, strategy, philosophy/values, and style.

You'll recognize your alignment (or lack of it) with board mission and strategy as you work through developing strategic goals, prioritizing your important work, and setting the direction for your nonprofit. When you all experience agreement about these essential things, your connections strengthen.

As you work together, you learn what each other values and how aligned you are. I'm sure you've experienced a time when you didn't all agree about something, and it became clear that values were clashing. Here's an example.

In 2020, when the COVID-19 Pandemic hit, the United States government developed several economic relief programs, one of which was Payroll Protection Program (PPP) loans. Tom, an executive director, called me for support when he faced a conflict with one of his board members, who happened to be the treasurer, about his nonprofit applying for one of these loans.

This nonprofit provides grief counseling and support to families. The budget was stable, and they had a reserve—at least until the pandemic hit and shelter-in-place orders impacted their operations. Tom presented the best form of a budget he could in this uncertain environment, and he showed how the PPP loan would be used. The treasurer strongly objected.

The argument against applying for the loan was that they had a good reserve. The treasurer felt they should not be competing with other nonprofits. Tom's position was they had an obligation to ensure services to their clients, and demand for services was unmet and growing. Why miss an opportunity to stabilize funding in such uncertain times? This was a conflict of philosophy or values.

How often do you agree or disagree with board members? This can be an indicator of your alignment if the issues are important. Don't assume your board members are aware of it. You all may take alignment for granted until there's an overt disagreement. From time to time, help your board members recognize you're all on the same page about essential things, appreciate it, and share how vital it is to your work together and your nonprofit.

Roles and Expectations

The most common issue I hear from executive directors about their boards is board members don't understand their roles and responsibilities. This is particularly challenging as younger nonprofits with "younger" boards are growing up and away from board members' having been active volunteers in the day-to-day operations.

We talked about this in the capacity chapters. The best way to clarify the distinction between the executive's role and the board's is to emphasize the executive leads the day-to-day management of the organization, none of which falls within the boards' governing role.

But challenges in this area often go deeper than you and your board members just knowing your roles. Board connection problems occur when board members' behavior isn't consistent with what you all thought you knew and understood.

A primary strategy for building your connections with your board chair and board members is to be intentional about clarifying who does what, the boundaries of your roles, your authority—for decision-making, signing things, spending money, etc., your expectations of each other. Talk about it together. This is how to go beyond this as a board capacity issue: delve into how board members envision and experience their roles personally.

Depending on the life stage of your nonprofit, this can be a lot more complex in practice. It's not productive to be rigid. It *is* productive to be clear! Express your expectations of your board members in a positive and constructive way. It can be a useful strategy to *ask* for what you want and expect. I don't mean you should beg. And you want to use a tone respecting who they are and what they have to give—they're volunteers, after all. And be sure you're realistic.

It's important to follow up on those conversations as needed and confront issues proactively, clarifying roles and expectations again. Your actions must be consistent with your agreements. And, if they're not, you need to deal with it. Work it out together. Your goal is reciprocity—each of you views and accepts each other's roles, or whatever you're working out, the same way!

Because relationships are complex, you all may need to remind each other about roles and boundaries from time to time. But, if there's not just a lack of understanding but a disagreement (or conflict), you'll need to put in more work.

Communication

How we communicate with each other encompasses many trust-building behaviors. There are three elements of your communication with your board to strengthen the connection: comprehensiveness, frequency and timeliness, and personalization.

You want to remind board members there are many of them and only one of you! I've known many executive directors who try to communicate in various ways with their boards because they feel they need to accommodate different board members' needs and wants. Not so! Remember, what should be your mantra: work it out!

Comprehensiveness

What type of information and how much does your board need and want from you? You can't answer this question if you haven't discussed it with your board members. In a context of mutual trust, you'll be willing to share the good, the bad, and the ugly without fear of reprisal.

I followed a founder who had been "buddies" with the board. These well-meaning people comprised what is referred to as a rubber-stamp board. As such, they accepted the level of information my predecessor chose to share. To his credit, he was open and transparent on the important things the board should know, but there were no regular reports. No format to emulate.

As we added new board members, the character of the board changed. They became more strategic. I learned some board members liked a lot of detail about our programs and finances, and others said, in effect, "Just give me the bottom line." I realized I didn't have the time to provide comprehensive reports for some and rework them for the "bottom line" board members who only wanted the equivalent of a bulleted list.

With the caveat I was always available one-on-one to answer questions, I arranged with my board chair dedicated time at a board meeting to discuss this. Board members "got it" right away and agreed on the form and type of reports they wanted from me routinely. We also agreed on some guidelines for what's urgent or important, so there were no surprises.

Executives meet their board members' expectations for communication in various ways: monthly written reports, weekly email updates, program staff attending board meetings for "mission moments" (a great practice, by the way). As part of the information you communicate, equip the board with the tools they need to evaluate organizational performance and your own performance. Another tip is to seek opportunities to remind and focus the board on the mission. This is the unifying force connecting you all.

There are no rules about this. Work it out together. Your connection with your board will grow.

Frequency and Timeliness

I'm sure you've experienced different board member needs for how often they want to hear from you. Timelines need to be clear with the board—be sure you're managing those expectations. How soon is a report back expected? Be specific.

Timeliness also refers to how long you may wait before reporting something, how fast you are at returning phone calls or emails, and your expectations of board members about the same. (You will be best served being proactive about agreeing on these expectations. You don't want anyone guessing about them.)

Personalization

As you're intentional about trust-building, you'll naturally get to know each other. As you do, be sure to address your individual communication preferences. Things like email communication, text messages, and even phone calls—these are all things people have preferences about.

An executive director expressed frustration with his board chair's lack of responsiveness to his emails. I suggested he talk with her about it and, when he did, he learned she preferred to communicate by phone and requested he call her instead of emailing. When he did, to his surprise, his calls and voicemails got quick responses.

This is about your preferences, too. And your needs. With mutual trust, you'll be free to ask for help and seek advice and support from board members when you need it.

This section covered the four factors research shows influence the board/executive relationship: executive assets, alignment, managing roles and expectations, and communication. As with the types of interactions and trust-building strategies discussed above, these factors provide additional ways you can build the connections you have with your board chair, board members, and the board as a whole.

In this chapter, so far, we've covered specific ways you can build your connections with your board chair, board members, and thus your full board. We must bust the myth what's professional is not personal and vice versa. Nonprofits are the places where people express and fulfill their passions. It's personal! The more *different* ways you work to build trust, the stronger trust in your relationships will be.

The action steps we've reviewed are useful in all kinds of situations—even when there's tension or conflict. But I know from experience you may need more.

What to Do When It's Disagreeable

Isabella shared tearfully with her executive colleagues in our group meeting a very hurtful interaction she had just had with her board chair. In a meeting with another board member about recruiting new board members, the board chair, Karen, dismissed Isabella's suggestions, leading with something like: "We are your boss. You shouldn't be involved in identifying potential board member candidates." The other board member clearly but calmly disagreed with Karen, which set her off, and a few minutes later, Karen actually yelled at Isabella.

At that point, Isabella stood up. "You are very angry," she said with all the composure she could muster. "I'm going to leave the room so you can calm down. We can continue our discussion when I come back. This yelling is not okay."

Isabella did some other things which will serve you in a challenging interaction. First, she became the adult in the room. She kept her cool and recognized the interaction wasn't about her; it was about Karen. She was firm in not tolerating bad behavior but demanding respect.

While out of the room, Isabella considered her options and decided what she would do, which did *not* include threatening, blaming, or becoming defensive. What helped her the most was keeping the focus of the conversation on the mission.

In addition to the tips you can learn from Isabella, there are four relationship-building principles and a few tips about getting help I want to share with you. These come in handy when things are tense or even ugly. They're approaches for building relationships that work.

What to Do about It: Apply Relationship-building Principles

Take Full Responsibility for the Relationship

Contrary to what you may think, your responsibility is not just 50 percent. When you take 100 percent responsibility for the relationship, you are modeling for the other person. One example of this is avoiding blame.

When we completed our merger and I stepped into the CEO role, I had executive leaders on my team I hadn't worked with before. They came into their positions by virtue of their roles in one of the partner agencies. I found my relationship with one of them was awkward and tense.

Our styles were different. In some cases, our values were different, I felt. While at a leadership conference, I approached one of the expert presenters and asked advice for strategies to deal with my executive leader. I shared examples of the interactions I found challenging. The first thing she said to me was, "What are you doing to perpetuate this relationship pattern?"

Her advice was all about my taking 100 percent responsibility for the relationship. I was taken aback by her challenging question but came to realize she was right to direct me to reflect on this. It changed my perspective about my executive leader, and I recognized how I *was* perpetuating some patterns in my interactions with her. This awareness enabled me to change (It made all the difference for me going forward—with staff and later even with my board members.)

Seek to Understand

Steven Covey gave us this strategy in his classic, *7 Habits of Highly Effective People*. This is simple but not easy.

You've probably heard the expression, "I messages." This refers to your describing to the other person what you are experiencing instead of leading with blame. An example is saying, "When you say, or do, _____, I feel _____," as compared to, "When you say, or do, _____, you make me feel _____."

Catch yourself before offering your interpretation of a situation or your point of view. Ask clarifying questions to understand the other person's perspective. Work to assess if the issue is organizational or interpersonal "chemistry."

And, critically important, don't jump in with "your side" until you have paraphrased back to the person what you now understand, to confirm you got it. People bring their own understanding and experience to a situation. Learn as much as you can before responding.

Check out Assumptions

We all make assumptions. We couldn't function if we didn't interpret what we observe, hear, and experience. To arrive at our interpretation, we move through a series of steps, some of which are unconscious. When we do, we frequently skip right over our awareness of our assumptions as we interpret our experience.

It takes discipline to stop and think it through. The warning sign is a feeling—usually one we don't like. It can be anger, hurt, frustration . . . When you experience a negative emotion in response to someone—a board member or your board chair, for example—try to identify what was said or done and then ask yourself: What else could it mean? How am I interpreting this? What other interpretations are possible?

It's best to ask the person directly for clarification but sometimes not possible. Try to check out your assumptions. And, of course, don't respond or act right away if you can avoid it.

Focus on Reciprocity

Ask yourself, "What can I give this person?" and "How can I put the other person first?" Small wins can make a big difference in how board members experience you and how they choose to respond to you. They are more likely to reciprocate if you give first.

I'm not talking about something big or expensive. Small acts can really matter. Examples of wins you can create for another person include acknowledgment, recognition, a unique opportunity to make a difference, a social experience, or visibility among colleagues. If you've done your work to get to know them, you'll be able to think of personal ways to give to them.

Another thing. Work on creating an "and" rather than an "either/or" solution. How can you approach the situation to both solve the problem and build the relationship? Hold out for a creative option; take your time.

What to Do about It: Get Help

Don't think because you're the executive director, you should be weathering a connection storm with your board chair or board member alone! Your job is stressful enough without having to deal with beyond-normal interpersonal tensions. You'll not only feel better, but you'll also be more effective in handling the situation if you have support. This can take many forms; here are three to consider.

Colleagues

Reach out to another executive director. Having someone who can listen and reflect back to you can bring a new perspective and comforting encouragement. This can be a phone call or an in-person meeting.

Find out if there's an executive director "roundtable"—a regular meeting of executive directors for mutual support and problem-solving—in your area. This is an excellent, proven-effective resource you want to be a part of, even if you don't have a connection issue. (I have an executive director Leadership Circle you can check out on the *Resources Page.*)

Board Member

If you have a trusting relationship with another board member or two, it may be appropriate for you to request a meeting. Approach this as a request for confidential coaching and mentoring. You're not looking to line up allies against anyone. This is for your professional development. Ask for support to help you with options for a plan of action or just to be a sounding board. Be sure you can trust the board member you approach will see it that way too!

Engage a Third Party

I've had an executive coach for many, many years. It has been so valuable! I encourage you to consider engaging a coach or finding a mentor, or both.

You may want to consider engaging a third party to meet with you and your board chair or board member—wherever the problem resides. This can be done early at the first sign of trouble or maybe as a last resort.

Jamar was the CEO of the board of a nonprofit equestrian service helping veterans with PTSD through a relationship with and riding horses. The board chair was the founder, Celeste, who led this nonprofit for many years and remained on the board after Jamar was hired. They just didn't see things the same way.

Celeste insisted Jamar was doing a great job and, despite the tension between them, things were going well. The rest of the board was invested in keeping both of these leaders happy. Jamar was frustrated with the seeming roadblocks he kept running into with Celeste. She disagreed with his ideas for improving programs and told him not to change how they did things. He often heard the equivalent of, 'That's not how we do it here.'

Often these conflicts would get resolved to Jamar's satisfaction but not without a lot of time and energy. The board members finally insisted they hire a professional mediator to help them work out agreements to significantly reduce this pattern of tension and conflict.

Later I heard from Jamar that the mediation really helped, and he and Celeste have a set of strategies for working things out.

What to Do: Identify Your Options

When proactive trust and relationship-building strategies aren't working, and you truly have someone impossible for you to work with, you still have options.

My executive coach taught me a strategy I offer you: identify five options. "What?!" you may be saying. "I don't have five options. I'm lucky if I have more than one: quit!" Trust me. You have at least five. I can get you started. <u>Beyond a choice to resign, do nothing.</u> I'm not recommending this necessarily, but it's an option. Now it's your turn.

Think through and write down your options. This exercise will remind you that you have choice and hope. The options you have are likely not ideal, but you can act from choice.

My heart aches for executive directors who have challenges with the interpersonal connections with their board chairs and board members. What lost potential for everyone involved!

Key Lessons

- Engage in diverse types of interactions to build trust.
- Get to know your board chair and board members.
- Strive for identification-based trust; make relationships appropriately personal.
- Meet with your board chair early in the relationship and regularly after that.
- Work out authority, roles, and boundaries with each other.
- Know and share your executive assets.
- Clarify communication preferences and gain agreement.
- Take 100 percent responsibility for each relationship.
- Seek to understand and check out assumptions.
- Get help if and when you need it.

Wrapping It Up

It's a cliché but true: <u>the best strategy is prevention.</u> <u>Invest time and attention in these critical connections.</u> <u>Work *on* the relationships, not just in them!</u> Love your board chair and board members. Apply what you learn here, and you'll have a board you love.

You know how to nurture your board and make strong connections. Think of the tree. Nurturing it keeps the canopy full and lush with the leaves connected to branches, creating a sturdy and healthy trunk.

This chapter focused on people and building the one-on-one connections between you and your board chair and you and board members. The strategies we covered for these one-on-one connections also apply to board members' one-on-one relationships with each other. There may be issues for you when board members don't get along with each other or don't work effectively together. You can draw on the strategies from this chapter to help.

Next, let's delve into the process side of board connection. Connection processes address the problems you have with the board because of board members' relationships collectively— the challenges arising when the board is not functioning as a strong team.

The trunk of the tree is a metaphor for a strong team. A strong board team is created when the connections you all have come together. Let's go to the next chapter.

CHAPTER FIVE

Connection: Process

"**H**alf the board—seven of them—stood up and walked out of the room!" As he told me this, David, the board chair, slammed his hands down on the table in frustration. The CEO, Michaela, looked at me dismayed, nodding her head. Their request of me came next—but let me set the context.

Michaela and David led Services for Special Children, a 134-year-old nonprofit with an array of services for children with developmental disabilities. Its history and focus, however, was on residential treatment programs. Over the prior three to five years, trends in its field of service were moving, slowly at first, but surely, toward in-home models of care. At a critical point financially, it faced some tough decisions about phasing out these historic and beloved services.

A key board committee, with Michaela, had spent months reviewing strategic options and the implications. The choices being recommended were embodied in their proposed new fiscal year budget. The recommendations were not a total surprise, having been discussed at a previous board meeting. The bottom-line choice was clear: close one residential program and implement a phasing out of the other three over the next two years.

At this critical board meeting, a motion to approve the proposed budget was introduced, and discussion ensued. After clearly not enough time, a board member called for the question. Misunderstanding how this "rule" works, the board chair and the board believed calling for the question automatically forces a vote, ending discussion on the spot. The board chair called for the vote. Eight board members voted for the proposed budget, and the other seven, who opposed it, walked out of the room.

And here we were. I didn't judge if this was a good or bad development. Clearly, David and Michaela hoped for more alignment among the board members or at least a creative compromise. They asked me to teach the board how to make decisions—a board capacity-focused solution. I convinced them the board needed to develop some key processes; agreements supporting collaborative and trusting connections were needed first. After doing that work together, the board members were ready to revisit the vote and, this time, they made a unanimous choice—united in what was best for Services for Special Children.

Last chapter, we talked about problems with your board rooted in one-on-one *people* connections and strategies to address them. You learned many of those strategies, such as building trust, apply to your key one-on-one board member connections: with the board chair, the board as a whole, and individual board members.

This chapter focuses on the strength and quality of connections *among* your board members—the process side of board connections. You probably experience problems with board connections along a continuum from mild to serious. The examples of board problems we'll delve into here can be avoided, mitigated, or solved completely by good board connection processes, like those making the difference for Services for Special Children's board. But first, something about you.

How Do I Fit In?

Before we delve into board challenges resulting from poor or lacking board connection processes, I want to clarify how you fit in. After all, this is about the board members' connections with each other, so you may be asking: What's the executive director's role? How do I fit in? In two ways.

First, while you're likely not a voting member of the board, you can and should be a member of the "team." That means you have strong connections with each of the board members and bring a critical perspective and essential information to board deliberations. You are, or at least should be, a powerful influence—and thus team member. If you're a voting board member, position alone won't give you this influence—strong connections will.

Second, you're a crucial catalyst for board development. Yes, this can be a delicate dance but, in many ways, e.g., asking questions, presenting issues, suggesting action, you are the "nudge" we talked about in Chapter One. When it comes to building connections between and among board members, you are—or can be—a key facilitator.

As you learn strategies below for what to do about engaging board members, building trust, and creating a well-connected board team, think about how you can work with the board chair and the governance committee's chair to implement them.

Your Board's Connection Processes

As with Special Services for Children, boards and executives often look to the board's people and process capacity to improve functioning or solve issues. Sometimes it's enough, but if the problem you're experiencing with your board is caused by connection dynamics among the board members, you'll need a good board *connection process* to resolve it.

The ability and willingness of each board member to build and nurture connections with the others are critical for your board. And the strength or lack of board members' interpersonal skills will spill over to impact the board's effectiveness as a group. You can mitigate some of those individual weaknesses with a sound board connection process.

It starts with correctly recognizing the problem is a board connection process issue. What to do about it is what this chapter is all about.

Let's consider some examples.

The Board Is Inefficient and Unproductive

When your board is not functioning well as a team, it takes longer to get things done, and there may even be a focus on the wrong things. If you want a productive board, you have to engage people, and engagement requires a connection. This plays out at board meetings and with committees. Problems with board members' interpersonal interactions in either of these groups take time away from the board's work at hand. Here are two ways I've seen this show up.

The first way is passive compliance on the board. An environmentally focused nonprofit working on energy-efficient solutions was growing significantly. The board needed to evolve with it. The board chair was a human resource professional. Because of her work experience, she frequently asked questions drawing the board into day-to-day operations, particularly related to staff.

Meetings were long and inefficient; things needing board attention just weren't getting done. The real issue underlying the board's ineffectiveness was the weak relationships among the board members and with this board chair. People were uncomfortable raising concerns with the board chair directly and didn't talk to each other about it either, so the dynamic causing the problem was "undiagnosed."

Instead of assessing the real issue as the target of change, the board decided it could improve meeting efficiency by reactivating the executive committee. They thought the executive committee could streamline the board agenda and deal with things they felt wouldn't need to go to the full board.

This structural—board capacity process solution—did not work. The executive committee soon became the platform for lengthy inquiries and discussions. Board members not on the executive committee began to feel marginalized. It added an unnecessary layer of work for both board officers and the executive director, and it didn't fix the ineffective and inefficient board meeting dynamics.

Another way poor connection among board members causes passive compliance, and thus inefficiency, is the resurfacing of issues or decisions—a board member raising an issue the board acted on already. Fellow board members or the board chair don't confront this breach of protocol because they're conflict-averse and haven't connected with the person or each other enough to feel okay objecting. With weak connections, they don't feel safe or comfortable challenging or confronting each other.

The second example of a problem fitting within board connection process is the interpersonal conflict between board members. Here's a story illustrating what I mean. A board member, Janet, shared her experience with a particularly challenging board member:

> *I chaired the committee working on our fundraising event. The committee had agreed one of the items would be in our silent auction and not the live auction typically reserved for the highest value items. One of the board officers not on the committee, Eleanor, had obtained the item. She was furious the item was not going to be in the live auction. She went off on me. She stated it better be a live auction item, 'or else.'*

In addition, Eleanor refused to follow up on other contribution commitments unless Janet complied.

This conflict was experienced by the entire fund development committee, and the time-sensitive work they needed to finish for the event was significantly impacted. Janet felt verbally abused by Eleanor. Turns out, beyond the committee, the interpersonal exchanges between Eleanor and other board members were also difficult and taking their toll.

As volunteers, board members don't sign up for this kind of experience. In addition to causing board work to be bogged down, people get hurt, frustrated, and angry. It doesn't take long for people to decide it isn't worth it and leave the board.

You're more likely to experience a roque board member when connections among board members are weak, and there's a crisis for your nonprofit. Board members genuinely intend to do good. Bad behavior is not intentional; sometimes, they can't help themselves. When situations create stress, anxious board members are more likely to vie for control in some way. That's a natural reaction in a crisis. Strong connections among board members create a team out of a group—a team that can provide support, counsel, and guidance when it is most needed.

I imagine you have a story from your own experience. Perhaps it's not a control or ego issue with a board member interfering with a constructive connection. Someone may just need attention and, thus, dominates board discussion or takes discussion off track. It can be subtle, but it still negatively affects board productivity.

Board Members Are Not Engaged

You may experience a disengaged board member in many ways. What seems to come up the most is absence. Absence from board meetings, committee work, and other contributions you may expect of your board, including financial, are common signs. Unfortunately, I've known boards and executive directors who tolerate this disengagement and even make excuses for it because of some "special" characteristic (major donor, special connections, past board service), deluding people into thinking the board member is too valuable to lose.

Besides absence, though, there are other signs of disengagement: arriving late or leaving early, asking irrelevant questions or offering out-of-sync comments because the packet wasn't read, scrolling email or text messages throughout, even chatting in side conversations during the meeting. In short, just because board members attend the meeting doesn't mean they're engaged!

Disengagement can be contagious. If the board is lax in managing itself in this way, it's ultimately very damaging. I've heard from executive directors that they fear they won't get a quorum because the pattern of attendance has been so poor. Instead of being a force for good, the board can actually have a negative influence.

There can be many reasons for the lack of board member engagement. Some are board capacity issues, but often it's because of weak connections among board members. What's at stake is board effectiveness and loss of the positive impact a fully engaged board can have.

If the board members have strong connections with each other, this is much less likely to be a problem. With strong relationships, board members care about each other, enjoy seeing each other, and want to come to board meetings to be with each other. Connections provide an incentive for attendance.

Board Members' Potential is Untapped

I'm sure you've heard about board members who get on the board and then hold back—they are waiting to figure things out and want to observe for a while before they speak up. Orienting new board members is the time to make the connections so crucial for board engagement. With the typical monthly board meeting, it can take a long time for healthy relationships to build. Working on a committee can help, but not with the full board.

Remember the financial services executive who was a museum board member I shared about in Chapter Three? His story was about waiting months to learn what it means to be a board member while he held back—observing versus engaging. Think of all the ways he could have added value which were lost during the twelve months he'd been on the board!

The board problems described above are all caused or exacerbated by weak connections among board members. In short, the board is not functioning as a team. We know effective boards are first effective teams.

Teamwork creating results requires connection among the members. Yes, the board chair and you as executive director are the key leaders, but *every* board member influences the board's group dynamic. Purposeful focus on creating a foundation of strong connections among board members yields powerful board results, advancing your mission.

Bringing people together as a dynamic group allows the board to realize each member's potential and the full board's potential. So, when dealing with a board problem, be sure to consider how weak or poor board member relationships may be contributing. If they are, the following tips will help.

What to Do about It: Engage Board Members

One of the critical strategies for building connections among board members is to ensure each board member is engaged with the board and its essential work. There are several steps you can take to achieve that.

Board member engagement begins with board orientation. Build connection into your board orientation system. There are several ways to do that, including ensuring your new board members meet all the other board members and have a board buddy. Make time at board meetings for new members to be introduced and for them to learn some personal things about each board member.

I have seven additional tips for promoting board member connection and engagement. Ideally, partner with your board chair to do these, but you can make a difference on your own with any of them. I suggest you make these regular board connection processes.

Make it Personal

Get to know your board members. Learn each person's interests, skills, connections, and so on. Be sure you understand why they care about your mission.

Show They Matter

Show board members how and why they matter and how and why the board as a whole matters. Share stories about the board's impact on your mission and the opportunities available for your board members to make a difference.

Get Aligned

Ask them how they want to be of service and help. Match what you learn about your board members personally with your board's important work and the opportunities available to board members.

Check In

It is particularly important to check in with board members from time to time—with your board chair but also on your own. One-on-one meetings are a great way to promote engagement. Learn what's going on with them.

Make Board Service a Win/Win.

Make sure your board members are getting something out of their board service. Don't take for granted that contributing to a worthy cause is enough. It's not just okay; it's desirable for board members to get something out of it, such as learning new things, developing skills, and making new connections.

Make it Fun

Not all board work has to be serious. Board members need chances to connect with each other and you personally. Work with your board chair to build in regular social time—at board meetings and a couple of times a year at a gathering designed just for that purpose.

Set Engagement Goals

Discuss and decide, with the board, what board member engagement looks like. Set goals and agree on how to measure the results and when. Then, monitor how you're doing.

Be intentional about engaging board members. It's an ongoing part of board development and essential to board member connection. The activities you do to engage board members are board connection processes.

What to Do about It: Build Connection into Your Board Recruitment System

Recruiting board members is not just about assessing if they have the profession and connections you're looking for. An effective board recruitment system prioritizes interpersonal fit with the executive director and other board members. You need to start assessing this from the very beginning.

In addition to information-gathering, build connection processes into your board recruitment. This generally starts with the executive director and board chair meeting with the person. Also, include a time when the prospect can informally interact with as many of the other board members as possible.

When I was CEO after our mergers, our board of seven prioritized building to a board of fifteen. In addition to meeting with my board chair and me and attending a board meeting, our prospects met with board members for an informal dinner. By the time our chosen candidates were elected, we already knew them and vice versa. Positive connections were formed. These board members were able to hit the ground running—no time was wasted.

What to Do about It: Develop the Board as a Team

The steps for building an effective team I cover below comprise the critical connection processes your board needs in place to avoid, mitigate, and resolve board connection problems and issues. Using them, your board members will connect with each other, effectively work together, and, most importantly, create positive results supporting your mission.

Being an effective team starts with strong, trusting relationships. Board member connections are the foundation for essential team dynamics: constructive conflict, commitment, accountability, and attention to results.

The tips we covered in Chapter Four for building your one-on-one relationships with board members also apply to board members' connections with each other. We talked about building trust. We reviewed factors that apply to influencing board members' relationships with each other: individual assets, communication, setting and honoring expectations, and alignment in style and purpose. Be sure to apply what you learned in Chapter Four here.

There are six connection processes needed to build your board as a team: establishing a strong foundation of trust, creating a shared vision for the board's work, developing intentional agreements, and building in accountability, acknowledgment, and assessment. Suggestions for how to tackle all of these comes next. What I'm sharing is evidence-based, what I've learned from my own experience and research and that of others—particularly the work of Deborah Pruitt, PhD. I strongly recommend you check out her work and get her book, *Group Alchemy* (available from the *Resources Page*).

Establish a Strong Foundation of Trust

Trust makes all the other strategies for successful team-building work.

The results of a board self-assessment done by a home health care nonprofit revealed board members felt they didn't know each other. The average tenure of this group of board members was six years. Even after all their time together, they didn't feel personally connected. In the self-assessment, several board members characterized their board experience as meeting monthly and getting business done, but without time to get to really know each other or the way each contributed to their nonprofit's work.

Remember identification-based trust? Board members need opportunities to get to know each other personally, which usually means outside of board or committee meetings. But, even during sessions, board members can use strategies to build and strengthen trust among them. All of the trust-building strategies you learned in the last chapter will work for your board members. In addition, here are two trust-building strategies particularly relevant for a group context.

First, create safety. If people don't feel safe, they won't share their ideas or concerns. They won't give feedback. Creating safety becomes more personal and important as the board develops as an effective team. Things board members can do, and you can too, to create safety include being vulnerable and authentic and being proactive in taking a risk rather than waiting to feel fully safe themselves.

Your board chair has a key role in creating safety among board members by inviting them to share—making it safe for them by asking questions and showing an interest in their views. But it isn't only up to the board chair. Every board member has a stake and responsibility to create safety for the others.

Second, value input and feedback. This helps create synergy and promote creativity. Board members demonstrate they value input and feedback by seeking to understand, asking questions, and then paraphrasing to check out their understanding; listening without interrupting; focusing on the idea or behavior, not the person; and avoiding evaluative words like "good" and "bad."

With a strong foundation of trust, the other connection processes we cover below for building your board as a team will be even more effective.

Create a Shared Vision and Goals

I'm referring here to a shared vision and goals *for your board.* In Chapter Two, we covered ways your board can organize itself around the roles it has supporting achievement of your nonprofit's strategic goals—establishing its own goals for the results it commits to achieving.

Your board's purpose is to advance your nonprofit's mission, but how? And how now? What results does the board need to achieve in the near future? In the discussion your board members have as they answer these questions, encourage them to answer one more: what kind of group do we want or need to be to achieve this?

Getting clear together about the results they want to achieve, how to self-organize to achieve them, and exploring together what kind of board they want to become, all build community, alignment, and connection— among board members and with you. Doing this work builds trust and promotes a shared identity for the board. As a result, your board will have its own vision and goals.

Knowing the impact they want to achieve enables your board members to do two other things: 1) help individual board members connect their personal "why" for serving your nonprofit with the board's work, and 2) collectively collaborate to achieve their vision for themselves as the board. Both of these build connections among the members, and your board will be on its way to becoming a powerful team.

After creating a shared vision and goals, your board is ready for the next team-building step.

Develop Agreements Intentionally

Relationships are built on agreements, which we all know from experience can be implicit or explicit. Whether or not the agreements your board members have with each other and with you are implied, they exist. The processes your board members use to create agreements are opportunities to build connections—and thus the team.

In my experience, board members are better at working out agreements about how they want to work together at board retreats than at regular meetings. For example, many boards easily accept the value of creating ground rules for themselves at an all-day retreat, but few create them for regular board meetings.

Agreements promoting board member connection and more efficient and effective board work include agreements about how the board will organize itself, such as committees, meeting frequency, who does what, expectations for reporting, and the scheduling and timing of expected deliverables.

Work to make your agreements as specific as possible. Talk it through. For example, what does "confidentiality" mean? You may find it helpful to proactively ask board members about some of these powerful words they all take for granted. They don't mean the same to everyone.

Because you work so closely with the board, I encourage you to work together in forming many of these agreements. You and your board members can decide which ones and how. Just creating agreements together strengthens your connections.

To exemplify this, let's consider a couple of typical board member agreements: rules of engagement and decision-making rules.

Rules of Engagement

Some board member agreements promoting connection are about conduct. Reflecting on and answering: how do we want to be together? Rules of engagement, or ground rules, are an example. Some common ground rules are:

- Let go of attachment to the outcome; be open-minded throughout the process.
- Come from your experience—"I" messages—do not speak for the group.
- Speak up; don't hold back opinions or concerns.
- Don't dominate the conversation.
- Assume goodwill, competency, and value.
- Honor confidentiality.

Decision-making Rules

Let's illustrate these with a story:

Following up on a board meeting discussion, board members and the CEO, Duong, were engaged in a lively email exchange, brainstorming ideas for attracting new volunteers and donors to their nonprofit. Duong eventually politely bowed out of the exchange, explaining a grant deadline he was working on did not allow him the time to comment on all the suggestions.

The board members continued the email discussion. Over the next couple of weeks, they formulated a plan, voted on it, and approved it. The board chair then presented the plan to Duong for implementation. He was furious! The board chair was taken aback and offended, and things went downhill from there.

They had made a decision without Duong's input. There was no clear agreement about how the decision would be made and by whom. The problem was the board members assumed his departing the discussion was, in effect, leaving the decision in their hands. Duong shares responsibility for this breakdown, too, for not clarifying his expectations or the next steps regarding the decision. This example also highlights how the executive director is a member of the team.

When trust and connections are strong, decisions are well-informed and thus better. Why is that? Decisions made as a board *team* are more grounded in reality because people have been more open about their views and perspectives.

While you and your board members can't anticipate how you'll want to make every decision, understanding key decision-making elements will facilitate agreement on a process when needed. Here are three tips to consider when creating board decision-making rules.

High Stakes or Low Stakes?

Determine if the decision is high stakes or low stakes. Closing a program is an example of a high-stakes decision. Agree on some criteria for defining high or low stakes.

Agree on the Voting Rule

For a high-stakes decision, you may want the vote to be unanimous (you all agree) or by consensus (most agree, and the rest agree they can "live with it.") These are win/win criteria. For low-stakes decisions, the typical board uses a majority, of a quorum, vote. This is a win/lose decision because some can disagree, but the motion will still pass.

Gather Information

Agree on how you're going to gather timely and appropriate information to use to make decisions. You won't meet everyone's needs, so having an agreement on this is essential. This is particularly true for you as the executive director because staff often do a lot of the information-gathering work.

From time to time, particularly for high-stakes issues, I recommend you and the board assess the decision-making process you used. An example is asking board members to agree or disagree with these statements:

- I was able to voice my viewpoint.
- I believe other board members understood my viewpoint.
- I believe I understood other board members' viewpoints.
- Whether or not I prefer this decision, I support it because the board came to it in an open, fair, and inclusive manner.

Again, the reason for working all this out is to build the board as a team—creating the connections among board members and you for board effectiveness and positive impact. You'll have expectations of each other, but sometimes one person's idea is not another's. Making agreements together about expectations not only helps an individual board member make choices about behavior or comments but empowers you to remind people gently if they violate an agreement—keeping it about "us" and our agreement versus "you." This helps build connections, too.

There are three more board connection processes that build your board as a team: accountability, acknowledgment, and assessment.

Create an Accountability Process

In this context, think of accountability as an agreement to track and follow up on what board members individually and collectively have committed to do. For the board as a team, it means having ways to measure progress on group goals and follow up with individual board members who have assignments.

When your board members make agreements, it's most effective to build accounting methods for the results right into those agreements. This provides a way to be accountable. Too often, accountability is skipped over—maybe because it's taken for granted or perhaps because no one understands how vital intentional agreement about accountability is to board functioning.

Building accountability methods into board agreements has the added benefit of ensuring you're all on the same page about what constitutes performance. It also puts the focus on results and not the person, which helps depersonalize performance. It strengthens your board as a team when what people are accountable for is straightforward as well as how it will be measured, and when.

For your board as a team, accountability also provides feedback on what's working and what isn't. And accountability applies to how board members behave with each other, such as honoring rules of engagement and their work results. Together, your board members learn and grow, further strengthening their connections.

Acknowledge Each Other

Acknowledgment should naturally flow from accountability. Too often, when asked to identify who has been thanked too much, board members in groups I've led respond with resounding silence.

As you and board members get to know each other, you become aware of each other's gifts and talents. Team members need to know each other to understand how each contributes to achieving the board's work. Acknowledging each other's contributions to achieving group goals strengthens all of you as a team and, as a result, the board, with you, will be more effective.

Claire, the new executive director of a small social service nonprofit, with her board chair Eduardo, worked hard on building trust and board member relationships. The board was made up of community leaders, most of whom did not want to fundraise. After all, they reasoned, that's why we have an executive director, right? Sound familiar?

Claire and Eduardo worked diligently to learn about each board member. As a result, instead of using a one-size-fits-all approach to board member fundraising expectations, they developed a very individualized approach to how each board member could support fundraising—especially in ways that didn't "feel" to them like they were fundraising.

Claire informed Eduardo regularly about what people were doing and the results. Eduardo, in turn, in board meetings acknowledged all the things—no matter how small—each board member did to support their fundraising goal. They connected around their goal through each person's unique talents, which were acknowledged in turn. With such an effective process, supporting step-by-step wins, they met their fundraising goals.

Appreciative Inquiry

Appreciative Inquiry is a proven-effective group management approach. Unlike problem-solving—assessing, diagnosing, and then finding a solution—Appreciative Inquiry says: find what works! When we remember what worked in a similar situation, we get back in touch with positive, empowering feelings. This gives us confidence and commitment to repeat the experience. Your board's acknowledgment practices are a form of Appreciative Inquiry.

Assessment

Assessment is the practice of stepping back as a group and answering the question: how are we doing? We talked about board self-assessment in Chapter Three. Here I'm referring to assessing how the board is working as a team; how is the board doing in accomplishing the agreed-upon board goals? This is different from assessing the board periodically on its overall governing practices and effectiveness.

The practices making up assessment in this context include revisiting actions and results, revising your approach as needed, celebrating successes, reconnecting to agreements, and renewing or creating new agreements and goals. This is the process, at its core, of updating the board's important work and moving forward as a strong team into the new, refreshed future you envision together.

Key Lessons

- Recognize culture underlies everything.
- Use the strategies provided to intentionally engage board members.
- Build personal connection into your board recruitment system.
- Develop the board as a team:
    - Build a strong foundation of trust.
    - Create a shared vision and board goals.
    - Develop agreements intentionally.
    - Adopt an accountability process.
    - Acknowledge each other and celebrate together.
    - Reflect and assess.

Wrapping It Up

Challenges you experience with your board may be due to issues with connections among board members. The ability and willingness of each board member to build and nurture connections with the others are critical for your board. To have a strong, effective board team, you and your board need to put in place good board *connection processes*.

We've covered several board connection processes: intentional board member engagement practices, connecting board members as part of your board recruitment system, building trust, and specific strategies you can use to build the board as a team.

A key way you build connections among board members is the process of creating agreements. As repeatedly fulfilling those agreements becomes part of how your board does its work, your board's culture is formed. Your board's culture is like a tree's root system: mostly hidden, but the foundation for the tree's strength and growth.

Your board's culture is one of the three dimensions of this model within which problems, challenges, and issues you experience with your board reside. You may need to go deeper than connections—to board culture—to discover what's really going on and what to do to create the board you love. Let's explore that next.

CHAPTER SIX

Culture: People and Process

"**W**e need to recruit board members who will raise money for us," James, the executive director of Unleash Capabilities, a nonprofit serving children with disabilities, told me. "Will you come to our board retreat and do a training on the board's role in fundraising and recruiting?" I agreed and did. The training was followed by a discussion among board members led by Alice, the governance committee chair, which was responsible for board recruitment.

Alice made several comments like: "We can't find people who are willing to fundraise for us." "The people here in Silicon Valley who could help us are just too busy." "We don't have the connections we need to find the right people for our board." All the while, her fellow board members were nodding their heads in agreement.

The consensus among the board members was clear. No one challenged this thinking. No one offered alternatives or considered how their beliefs were blocking their success. They said the ability and willingness to assist with fundraising was a key new board member criterion. But, without openly talking about it, they were dismissing the possibility of it happening. From their actions and comments, it was evident they gave up on this criterion in practice.

They moved on to discuss other criteria they felt empowered to act upon—the deeper implication being an unspoken expectation of success with those.

This is an example of how beliefs and assumptions—elements of board culture—influence board performance. The third dimension of our model, and often unrecognized cause of board problems, is the board's culture. For board development efforts to work, sometimes we need to identify underlying cultural factors influencing, or even driving, what's going on.

You'll hear this again in this chapter, but it's a critical point. Your board's culture is manifested in the behaviors of your board members, individually and collectively. Their interactions reflect the culture often despite the values and results they claim to be committed to or strive for. This is why this dimension of our model is covered last—it's the deepest.

As I pointed out at the end of Chapter Five, board agreements and processes practiced over time become part of your board's culture. Again, it's what's *practiced* that matters. Culture is "the way" of your nonprofit, but also something everyone takes for granted.

Like any group or organization, each board has a unique culture evolving over time. Your board's culture is like the roots of a tree. A large established tree has an extensive root system, while a younger tree has a developing one. Root systems are hidden, and they are the foundation of the entire tree. Everything feeding the tree comes through those roots. Board culture is pervasive and strong, but board members, and you as the executive director, are often unaware of it and its influence.

Culture is a complex and expansive concept. Our understanding of culture as it applies to organizations, and groups within organizations, is often attributed to Edgar Schein, who defined and elaborated on it from his research in the 1980s. (Edgar Schein. 1985. *Organizational Culture and Leadership,* available from the *Resources Page.*)

Paraphrasing Schein, culture is a pattern of a group's shared beliefs and assumptions and the behaviors flowing from them. Those patterns develop as the group, i.e., your board, acts to achieve its purpose. As a result of those actions, group members learn what works or doesn't, and their beliefs, assumptions, and behaviors are reinforced. As the patterns become ingrained in the group, they become unconscious—the proverbial "just the way we do things."

In case you're wondering what your role as executive director is, or can be, in shaping the board's culture, remember you are a member of the "team." As such, you bring an essential perspective and are in a position of influence with the board. By noticing where there are breakdowns or lack of alignment between your board's stated intentions and its actions, you can provide the nudge we discussed in Chapter One—you can be the catalyst for change.

As with your board's capacity and connection dimensions, there are people and process aspects to the problems you may encounter because of your board's culture. Board culture problems can be due to the assumptions and values board members have collectively adopted, the people aspect, or their patterns of behavior together.

As I mentioned in the Introduction, the strategies you learn here for addressing your board's people or process culture problems are basically the same. As a result, this chapter is organized differently than the others. We'll cover examples of the people aspect of board culture problems and then the process aspect, but all in this chapter. After reviewing those examples, I'll share the evidence-based strategies you can use to address them.

You'll see these strategies have slight differences, or nuances, depending on if you're dealing with a belief or assumption, a value, or a process—but the overall framework of the approach to addressing board culture problems is the same.

Your Board's Culture: People

People bring their own world views, beliefs, assumptions, and values to everything they do. But it's the beliefs or assumptions your board adopts *as a group* that become elements of its culture. They underlie actions your board takes, even though board members may be unaware of how shared beliefs and values are influencing them. For example, does your board assess financial position with a perspective reflecting beliefs of scarcity or abundance? How risk-averse is your board when deliberating opportunities or challenges?

Board Member Beliefs and Assumptions

Problems with board culture arise when group beliefs and assumptions get in the way of board effectiveness. Let's look at some examples, starting with the story opening this chapter.

156

James' nonprofit, Unleash Capabilities, was small, with ten staff, most of whom provided in-home services to the children they served. They didn't have the resources for a professional development director or special fundraising staff. Their services were primarily government-funded, and year after year, the board members set a goal to reduce what they considered "dependence" on it.

Even though already stretched thin, James took on fundraising. Board members agreed to help. Their idea of helping was to recruit new board members with fundraising leadership experience. For at least two years, fundraising experience was a new board member criterion. When it came to identifying and finding people to fill empty board seats, though, the scenario described at the opening of this chapter was repeated over and over again.

Underlying this cycle was a problem with the people aspect of this board's culture: the beliefs and assumptions board members were making about finding the board member prospects they needed and wanted for fundraising. Occasionally, they heard each other restate the limiting belief: "We can't find people who are willing to fundraise for us." But they were unaware how much of an obstacle it was. James recognized it but didn't know what he could do about it.

Let's look at another example. Consider this assumption I've heard many times: "We will lose continuity and valuable board members if we have term limits." Resistance to adopting term limits for board members is common. The board problems it can create are several: lack of diversity, group thinking, inertia, lack of innovation in strategies, and lack of vision.

Board Member Values

Let's consider another problem caused by the people side of board culture—in this case, a problem created by board member values.

Elizabeth, the new executive director, of a synchronized swimming club, reached out to me. During her first two months on the job, she made it a point to meet one-on-one with every board member. By the time she called me, she had also participated in two board meetings. She was an experienced executive director, and she was concerned her board members didn't seem to understand their roles and responsibilities.

The club was a membership nonprofit. Their mission was youth development and all it implied. The bylaws required every board member to be a club member in good standing. When Elizabeth was hired, all the board members were parents of the youth in the program or youth alumni, although board members were not required to be.

Their primary source of revenue was bingo. While the mission focused on youth development, the net funds raised were mostly spent on scholarships for youth who were candidates for their exclusive championship swimming program, regardless of *ability* to pay. Elizabeth shared that the head coach frequently articulated the program's goal as building athletes for the Olympics, notably not youth development.

As the executive director, Elizabeth began reallocating their considerable resources to other programs serving more disadvantaged youth who were not necessarily champion swimmers. Club members complained to board members, and

Elizabeth found herself defending her actions. She worked hard to educate the board about the risks to their nonprofit of the pattern of spending and focused attention on the one, more exclusive program. As issues came before the board, Elizabeth noticed board members frequently asking, "What would our members want?" instead of, "How does this advance our mission?"

The cycle of board decision-making driven by the unrecognized valuing of members over mission resulted in an IRS investigation challenging their tax-exempt status. They had accumulated significant excess revenue and were not, apparently, investing it in the youth-serving activities Elizabeth was promoting.

Even after training in their roles, responsibilities, and legal duties as board members, board decisions consistently reflected their valuing of members above mission. Elizabeth shared this conclusion with me after she resigned. This insight came to her after reflecting on all she had observed and experienced over the fourteen months of her tenure as the executive director.

This board's culture included a shared value which unfortunately undermined rather than advanced their mission. But, as with many cultural elements, this shared value wasn't recognized as a driver of board action.

Board Diversity

We know from research a lot of boards desire to be more diverse but are unable to get results. We talked about diversity when discussing board recruitment in Chapter Two, and I now want to get into more detail because I find problems with board diversity are often due to a board's culture.

Lack of board diversity is a board culture problem when your board members collectively don't value it. As we discussed above, shared values drive board behavior. Without a shared value, the people side of board culture, your board's actions in certain areas may be weak and ineffective.

Board member assumptions also get in the way of building a diverse board. For example:

- "We're only doing this because funders are promoting it."
- "We have great board members now and don't need more."
- "We're not discriminating, and we're really trying. We just can't find good candidates."

Board members are likely unaware of these beliefs and assumptions and may even deny them if asked. Or they may believe they are really true. Perhaps they just don't know how to explore why what they're doing isn't working. Board members could suspect conflicting values among themselves regarding diversity, equity, and inclusion and avoid discussing it because of expected discomfort dealing with underlying issues of racism or privilege.

Or they are simply clueless. Shared values, beliefs, and assumptions among board members are part of the board's culture, whether board members are aware of them or not. Applying our model, they make up the people side the board's culture dimension. If they are aligned with the shared mission, they will advance your work together. If not, they are the often-hidden source of board problems.

Your Board's Culture: Process

Like beliefs, assumptions, and values, your board's culture is manifested in its processes (the consistent ways it acts), norms, and traditions. Do board meetings start and end on time? Where do people sit? Does the board celebrate milestones and, if so, how? The implications of these examples of board norms and traditions are probably not as significant as the implications of other elements of your board's culture (such as those influencing board diversity) when deeds are inconsistent with stated intentions.

These processes may be intentional and documented like those discussed in Chapters Three and Five. Or they may be unconscious. When they are habitual, you can recognize them as elements of your board's culture.

Board Meetings and Inclusion

We know many boards intend to be more diverse—in many ways—yet nothing changes, or they just don't take effective action. If a board truly values creating a diverse board, there may be process aspects of the board's culture getting in the way. Traditional ways of doing things, such as board meeting practices, may not foster a culture of inclusion, and inclusion—going beyond a seat at the table—is a result of when and how your board acts.

Norms failing to foster inclusion can become barriers for people of color, those who are disabled, or others who are different from your board members. Research has identified several. (Merryn Rutledge, "Overcoming Hidden Barriers to Board Diversity and Inclusion," available from the *Resources Page.*) Let's consider some examples.

Meeting norms can pose significant barriers to inclusion. What time of day does the board meet? How does the meeting schedule influence a potential board member who works? What about the needs of a single mom who has childcare drops offs and pickups to manage, not to mention childcare costs to cover her attendance at the board meeting?

Location is another board meeting norm, possibly posing a barrier to inclusion. Is it systematically excluding someone who doesn't have a car? Is there public transportation making your board meetings accessible to certain populations at reasonable hours? How might your board retreat present barriers to inclusion?

Board members may consider conference call technology an accommodation, but it can also be a barrier to inclusion. For example, is the meeting facilitated with regular pauses and invitations for input from the caller, or is it assumed the person will be extra assertive to be heard?

The use of technology such as board portals assumes enough access to a computer and a certain comfort level with it. An older potential board member or disabled person may struggle, as may a parent whose child also needs access to the single household computer.

Accountability: Words Versus Deeds

Let's revisit James and his board. For at least two years, James presented a fundraising plan to the board during its annual budget development. He discussed with board members the need for their help and how they could make the difference in fundraising success. Every year, the finance committee recommended, and the board adopted, the fundraising plan James presented as an integral part of the annual budget. The plan included specific goals and action items for board members.

Consistently, board members—without dissent—said they would implement their part of the plan: individually contribute, help James with donor identification and cultivation, and recruit some new board members with fundraising experience. Just as consistently, they failed to follow through. But every year, they assured James it would be different.

James' board members were saying one thing but doing another. Yet, they failed to recognize this disconnect. A board with a strong norm of holding themselves accountable would have a different result. For this board, *not* being accountable for fundraising commitments was their norm: It's okay to say we'll fundraise and not follow through. This is another example of a problem with the process aspect of board culture.

Board Member-staff Interaction

I had the opportunity to work with the board members and CEO of an environmental advocacy organization for several months. As a result, I observed many board meetings. I couldn't help but notice several times a board member would reference a conversation with a staff member. Rather than information flowing to board members via the CEO, there was quite a bit of board member/staff interaction. Most of it related to the work of board committees and, in those cases, was not uncommon— particularly for a large nonprofit like this one. But some of the information was clearly about problems staff were bringing directly to board members about a variety of things.

I finally checked in with the CEO, LeeAnn, about it. Clearly frustrated, she told me she had given up trying to change this pattern of board members' behavior—not only responding to one-on-one approaches from staff but encouraging them. She shared board members felt strongly about having direct communication with any staff member no matter the topic. This board norm had been practiced over several years—even before LeeAnn's tenure. She said the board members argued this pattern of behavior was consistent with the board's responsibility for oversight.

This was unusual in my experience but a striking example of a process element of board culture. An important point is not to judge this as good or bad, particularly without openly considering if this pattern was working or not working for this board. Was this a shared value contributing to the board as a cohesive team? Was it impeding or aiding the board's ability to advance the mission? Given LeeAnn's distress and the risk this norm posed to their board/executive relationship's strength, I saw this was problematic.

I could tell many more stories about board problems rooted in board culture—both people and process issues. In fact, many of the problems we've discussed in this book could have a board culture element to them. Here are a few other board problem areas you may have experienced or heard about from colleagues that likely have a board culture element: board member engagement, risk tolerance, devil's advocate questioning, consensus-driven decisions, open inquiry, change, innovation, board member openness to learning, and leadership development.

What to Do about It: Your Board's Culture

Given how complex board culture issues are, problems you have with your board's culture likely have elements of both people *and* process. In this section, you'll learn steps to help you identify and address both. Remember the roots of the tree. You can't see their complexity, how deep they are, or how broad. Your board's culture is the same.

Most group culture evolves over time without clear intention. And it's not always consistent with what group members espouse. What matters is what people *do* consistently—your board members' habits. This is critical to keep in mind as you work together to change something that is in the roots, in the board's culture. Intention is a place to start, but it is consistent action that's required for results.

The strategies below draw on my experience but also on Deborah Pruitt's model for Group Alchemy (available from the *Resources Page*) because it's evidence-based and it works. The simplicity of the strategies and steps belies the challenges inherent in working to change beliefs, values, or behaviors. This may be simple, but it's not easy. Still, consistent and collective attention to these habits will yield great results in accomplishments and satisfaction for everyone involved.

Changing elements of your board's culture mimics any organizational change effort. If your board members think and experience everything as just fine, nothing is going to change. And, like any organizational change effort, sometimes it's easier than others; but sometimes the issues are deeper and more complex. For example, board members changing the time of their board meetings may be a quick and easy decision; but maybe not. It depends on the people involved and how important "the way we do things" is for them.

You and your board can take six steps to address board problems based on beliefs and assumptions, values, norms, or traditions. These steps comprise a board culture change management process, and you will see the similarities with the strategies for creating an effective team we covered in Chapter Five.

The time and effort it will take to fully implement these steps depend on the board culture problem being tackled. Things like how long it has been going on, how personal it is for some board members, and how clear and compelling the desire for change will influence the process and the result.

The six steps I cover below are:

1. Awareness—discover what's hidden
2. Vision—define the desired outcome
3. Planning—decide what needs to be done to achieve the goal
4. Accountability—agree on how the board will measure results for itself and for individual board members
5. Assess progress and adapt—repeating this cycle as needed
6. Appreciate and celebrate—this should be done throughout all the above steps

In each situation, realize these strategies are as much principles for how to explore and address the problems as they are specific tactics. Every board's culture is unique; adapt them, let them guide you, but don't skip any of them. Let's review each one.

Awareness: Reveal What's Hidden

I had the opportunity to work with the board of a historical society in a moderately sized rural community. There were ten members and no paid staff. Like James' board, these board members shared limiting beliefs about recruiting new board members.

As a result of our initial work together, they recognized the need to transition from a so-called "working board" to a "governing" one. They expressed frustration with their lack of progress in identifying new board member prospects, despite trying for several months. Their board retreat focused on developing a plan to attract several new board members to create a governing board. Some of the board members could transition to only volunteering in the society's operations per their preferences.

The process we used is an example of how you can approach changing or eliminating limiting beliefs or assumptions from your board's culture. Their first step was to become aware of them.

We're all familiar with these limiting beliefs:

- The earth is flat.
- The sun revolves around the earth.
- Humans can't run a mile in under four minutes.

The reason limiting beliefs like these changed is because someone dared to question why things were the way they were. This applies to changing your board's beliefs, too. The process of becoming aware can be triggered by someone challenging the way things are, causing a reassessment of the status quo, whatever the issue is.

In the case of the historical society, I was in a position, as the facilitator, to question the board. I asked each board member to answer this: when you think about recruiting new board members, what comes to mind? Asking a question like this can cause your board members to reflect on what they're thinking and even feeling about the problematic issue.

The shared beliefs of the historical society board members were reflected in the following comments:

- "We're small—we can't attract influential community members to our board."
- "Only people who love history would be interested in serving on the board of a historical society."
- "Our mission is narrow in scope and not as compelling as others; we can't compete."

It was clear to me they were unaware of how these limiting beliefs got in the way of their recruiting success. One of the tricky things about beliefs or assumptions is, like other elements of your board's culture, people are unaware of them and their role.

By surfacing their beliefs, these board members completed this first step: going deep enough to become aware of and identify these board culture elements. Your board can uncover hidden assumptions or beliefs by asking questions to reveal them. You can even ask directly: What assumptions are we making about [fill that in for your board]?

It's often helpful to have the assistance of an outside consultant, or to conduct internal surveys, and to ask provocative questions such as those posed here. It's important to create an open atmosphere—the safety we talked about—so everyone can freely flush out the quiet, private thoughts that shape what's seen as possible.

If you're dealing with a value, you may need to go even deeper. The conversation may be more complicated because values can be harder to recognize and articulate than beliefs or assumptions. Values may not be so much about what board members are thinking, such as beliefs and assumptions, but about the motivating factors underlying board member behavior. This may take more time. Discussing values is very personal, and it can require more sensitivity in managing the conversation than a discussion of beliefs or assumptions.

Here are some strategies you can use to reveal values:

- Identify the disconnect between what is said and what is being done. An example is boards wanting more diversity but aren't getting results. A question to help focus this discussion is: Why? Ask yourselves: Why aren't our actions or results consistent with what we say we will do or want to achieve?
- To go deeper, discuss how what board members are doing versus saying is serving the board now? What does it help to happen? How is it getting in the way?
- Ask: what's frustrating you?

The problem may be with a board norm or tradition. Again, there must first be awareness. It can start with someone questioning the status quo, sharing an observation of an inconsistency, or just asking "Why?" about a board practice or tradition. Is this working for us? Is it working for all of us? If not, why? The task is to reveal the hidden understandings and agreements supporting what isn't working.

For example, if your board is stuck, as many are, with inadequate progress on creating a diverse and inclusive board, start by examining why efforts are failing. There are numerous ethnic-specific nonprofits in our community, and other boards can learn a lot from them. Raising awareness on the board can open possibilities such as reaching out to ethnic-specific nonprofits, which your board members may not have considered.

To raise awareness and reveal what's hidden, be open to brainstorming, check in with each other, and openly share thoughts about the questions. Make it safe for everyone. From the chapters on board connection, you know now you need trust among you and the board members to do this. And, you now know how to build it. Circle back to those strategies if your board isn't ready for the deeper discussions required to change its culture.

Don't edit or evaluate what people share. Encourage people to speak up about whatever comes to mind. Take good notes of those conversations. It may take a while for themes or insights to emerge. Don't rush the process, either. Depending on the issue you're dealing with, this could take conversations over a couple of board meetings, if not more.

What's particularly challenging about this first step is recognizing its value and making time for it among all the other things your board is doing. Again, easier said than done. It's my experience once a board has the opportunity to surface and recognize an issue as an element of its culture, board members are willing to make the effort to do something about it.

As I mentioned, having a third party facilitate this can be very helpful and expedite the process if it's a touchy issue for your board. You don't want your board to lose momentum—there are more steps to take. Again, your goal in this first step is to collectively become aware of beliefs, assumptions, values, norms, or traditions getting in the way of the results your board wants to achieve. Remember, you can be the nudge that gets all this started.

Vision: Describe The Desired Result

When you're dealing with limiting beliefs or assumptions, the first part of this next step is to test the truth of the statements. Once board members are aware of their limiting beliefs or assumptions, they need to ask themselves: Are these real? Test each statement. Is it true? Additional questions to consider are:

- Where is the evidence this is true?
- Is it true for us? Now?
- What could it mean for us if it isn't true?

Board members may have direct experiences reinforcing their limiting beliefs but, if things are going to change, they must be open to challenging them—are they always true? For the historical society board, this conversation was an eye-opener, and they helped each other consider other possibilities. As we went through the limiting beliefs, the board members began to realize how much of a barrier they were.

This is the initial part of creating a vision. It makes it possible for the positive vision of what the board wants to create to emerge. After testing their limiting beliefs, the historical society board members created positive statements of what they wanted their reality to be. They created a shared vision.

Here are some of the affirmations the historical society's board members created, forming their vision:

- Many kinds of people from our community are interested in serving on the board of a historical society.
- Our mission is compelling and draws just the right board member prospects to us.
- We have many connections to explore, and new opportunities are opening up daily.

These questions are compelling: What do we want to create together? What do we want to change, and what will it look like when we do? At this step in the process, it shouldn't be too difficult for the board to articulate the result it wants to achieve—the vision of what will be different and how.

Jasmine, the executive director of a day center for those with dementia, worked on recruitment with her tiny board. She told me of their desire to have board members connected to the two primary ethnic communities they served, but that, to date, they had failed. Her few remaining board members had a pattern of reaching out to four or five business and membership groups when recruiting. As with many boards, these board members clung to their comfort zone.

They got to the point of recognizing this traditional way of recruiting needed to change (awareness). Taking this next step, they asked questions such as those suggested above. They connected in a very authentic way to the reason a diverse board mattered and committed to a vision: to add three new board members, but only people of color from the communities they identified, over the following six months.

Like them, create a vision you can measure so you'll know when you achieve it. In the next step, I'll share what they did.

Planning: Agree on What to Do

After creating a vision together of what you want—what change looks like for your board—the next step is to design and agree on the process you'll use to create it. Because there is an infinite number of possibilities for what may need to be different, it's impossible to delve into all the many options for processes to use. But, working from a foundation of trust (without which I doubt the issue would have come to light at all), you can be confident you'll all come up with what to do, or at least try first.

Here are some suggestions for how to come up with ideas for how to proceed:

- Brainstorm.
- Remember and draw on past successes.
- Present a new problem to solve—it helps reveal and test assumptions.
- Ask colleagues what works for them.
- Seek expert advice.

All of this takes commitment. For your board, it means a commitment to learning and development for itself, requiring a desire on the part of each board member to create and contribute to being the most effective board possible. This points us back to the people side of board culture: having people who share the value for doing this kind of development work. One of the most essential elements of a board's culture is valuing the board itself; commitment naturally follows.

Once they created their vision for the historical society board described in their affirmations, they committed to practicing

173

them—on their own and together—whenever they thought about new board member recruitment. If your board is dealing with limiting beliefs and affirmations, it may be tempted to skip the new practices. It may feel awkward and a bit too "woo woo" for you, but I assure you this works. Here's what the president of the historical society had to say about it:

> *Our work on identifying our 'mindsets' [beliefs] and the assignments to restate and practice them helped me reset my restrictive thinking about finding board prospects. I am much more comfortable approaching prospects since shifting my mindset to be open to possibilities.*

They used their vision to eliminate their limiting beliefs, opening up a whole array of possibilities regarding the backgrounds, professions, and spheres of influence they then added to their new board member criteria. Those criteria—the descriptions of the characteristics they wanted in new board members—formed another dimension of their vision. Remember, though, your board's culture exists in what people do, not just what they say. It lives in the practices. Within six months, they added four new board members, each of whom met more than one of their strategic criteria.

With coaching, the day-center board used two strategies to reach out beyond their comfort zones and find new, diverse board members. First, each board member created a diagram, a map, of personal connections. They intentionally expanded their thinking beyond the groups of people they typically approached—known friends, family, business associates—to people they didn't personally know and new groups such as school alumni and churchgoers.

Among those, they identified a list of people who they didn't know directly but who were part of the communities they wanted to reach. Then they did the equivalent of cold calling to request help with their goal. This was a stretch for each board member and clearly a diversion from their norms and traditional way of recruiting. But they needed to change the pattern, and it worked.

As you can see from these two examples, what to do to change a part of your board's culture will vary widely. Use the suggestions above as needed but work together to develop your unique plan with actions to achieve the vision you create.

Accountability: Measure Results

Lack of accountability underlies many board culture problems. In these cases, board members have an implicit agreement that it's okay not to do what was promised, not to follow through, and the board just accepts it as part of the reality of volunteer boards. In my experience, few boards have created explicit agreements about how board members will hold each other accountable, spelling out what will happen when board members don't do what they say they'll do and how the board will follow through with it.

A private middle school's board members were frustrated with their progress on two key strategic goals. They agreed on the goals and assigned ownership to two board committees, finance and governance, at a board retreat. After three months, a progress report on the goals was on the board's meeting agenda. It turns out, neither committee had made any progress on the goals; in fact, neither had even discussed them.

Reluctant to enforce expectations on their volunteer colleagues, the lack of progress was basically ignored. The board chair didn't approach either of the committee chairs to even discuss it. In addition, the goals, as initially stated, were not measurable, and there were no timelines attached to them, so there was no framework for accountability or clarity of expectations.

Ideally, establishing and practicing your accountability process—your accountability agreements—leads to accountability becoming an element of your board's culture. Accountability agreements include the board as a whole clarifying expected results, by when, and by whom. Accountability agreements should also include defining reporting processes. Committing to a structure for accountability models the board's commitment to it as a value as well.

In addition to creating accountability frameworks for group-level goals and assignments, I recommend boards develop an accountability process for dealing with individual board members. This would apply to any board member who commits to doing something and doesn't fulfill it, including committee chairs. Here are five steps to consider, or something like them, when the problem is with an individual board member, and the issue is important enough to warrant a response:

1. If someone has not met a commitment or followed through on whatever the person is accountable for, the first step is for another board member (preferably someone directly involved, such as a committee chair) to call and give a gentle reminder

The board member should inquire about what's going on, explore the reasons, and discuss options for moving forward, if applicable. Ask what help is needed and clarify and define expectations and commitments.

2. If the problem continues and the person again doesn't meet expectations as agreed, have a second conversation, making another inquiry, as in step one.

3. If the problem continues, one of the following options may be followed, depending on the issue and past experience with the board member:

    a. Consult with the relevant board committee chair, if not already involved.

    b. Consult with the board chair.

    c. Discuss the matter in an executive session of the board.

    d. Agree on an action plan.

4. Implement the action plan, which commonly would involve the board chair having a conversation with the offending board member— giving the person a "last chance" to tell the story and commit to an agreed-upon course of action or inaction. The key is agreement.

5. If the person continues to make agreements and does not keep them, it may be appropriate to follow the board member termination process as stated in your bylaws.

If this process seems harsh to you, remember effective boards are effective teams. Accountability is a critical characteristic and value for an effective team. No one likes to confront a colleague with an accountability issue. Still, with a process in place all board members have agreed on, it depersonalizes the process and helps facilitate quick and painless resolution. Establishing an accountability framework for the culture change vision the board creates is an essential step for success.

Whether you're addressing board member beliefs, assumptions, and values or board norms or traditions, there are two more steps to fixing a board culture problem.

Assess Progress, Adapt, and Repeat

This step is straightforward if you have an accountability framework in place, i.e., ways to measure and assess progress on the goals representing the vision. Have they been reached and, if not, why not? This is an iterative process you and your board members have experienced with prior planning work. It's just likely you haven't applied it proactively to elements of your board's culture.

The day center board put milestones in place and checked in monthly at board meetings about the progress being made. Paying attention helped keep their vision of a diverse board top of mind. In less than six months, they connected with, assessed, and elected four new board members meeting their diversity goals as well as other strategic criteria.

Once the middle school board created its accountability framework for each of its board action goals, they successfully managed any glitches that came up and accomplished all they set out to do.

This step is about implementing your accountability framework or process, evaluating the results, exploring why things didn't work out the way you all thought, and making adjustments. In effect, you are repeating the steps: becoming aware of what's going on, creating a revised vision, setting measures in place for accountability, and evaluating progress when the time comes. When you routinely following these steps, you're developing a learning organization that holds accountability positively—not in the more common punitive way.

Celebrate and Appreciate

The key to this step of the process is to be intentional. Put a placeholder at various times on the board's agenda to celebrate its successes and appreciate everyone in some way. This builds and maintains momentum. Do this throughout this process.

Institutionalize the Process

Once your board has learned from and experienced this process, your goal is to build it into your ongoing board practices. In other words, work to make it part of your board's culture—a habit. While you want everyone to feel safe raising an issue at any time, you also want to create a way to make a check-in process routine—a common and regular practice—for your board. For example, build into your board meetings a time for checking in about how things are going. Perhaps you put it on board agenda's once a quarter and make it part of your board retreat agenda year after year.

For more insights about how to approach, identify, and change problems with your board's culture, I recommend you check out

Deborah Pruitt's *Cycle of Renewal* in her book *Group Alchemy: The Six Elements of Highly Successful Collaboration* (available from the *Resources Page*). It covers the above steps and more.

You can wait for a problem rooted in your board's culture to surface, or your board can be more intentional and proactive about it. Ideally, you and your board have created an ongoing practice of checking in about how things are going and doing something about issues arising as a result. Practice inquiry rather than blaming. You now have insights to help you recognize problems driven by some aspect of your board's culture and what to do about them.

Key Lessons

- Recognize the roles of people and processes underlying your board's culture.
- Commit to diversity, equity, and inclusion and commit to *practices* that instill these values in your board's culture.
- Go deeper to identify board culture when it's the actual cause of a problem with your board.
- Use the six steps to address issues caused by your board's culture:
  - Raise awareness.
  - Describe the desired result and commit to it.
  - Agree on what to do to achieve it.
  - Be accountable; measure results.
  - Assess progress, adapt, and repeat.
  - Celebrate and appreciate.
  - Institutionalize the process.

Wrapping It Up

We have explored the third and last dimension of the model: culture. Board culture includes the beliefs, assumptions, and values your board members collectively, but likely unconsciously, use when making decisions and taking action. It also includes the patterns of the board's actions and behaviors that eventually become so "second nature" they make up board norms and traditions.

You probably noticed that as we moved through each dimension of this model, each goes a bit deeper into your board's characteristics and how board members work together. Like the roots of a tree, your board's culture is the foundation for everything flowing into its connections and capacity. These three dimensions of your board are interdependent—no one exists without the others. And remember, whatever you experience with your board will fit in one of the dimensions.

In the next chapter, we'll tie this together considering how board problems you experience may span all three dimensions. You now have tips and strategies for addressing the issues you experience in each of them. The next chapter aims to help you recognize the interdependence of the dimensions and have confidence that focusing on even one will make a difference. You'll be empowered to take action. As a result, you'll love your board!

Capacity
- People
- Process

Connection
- People
- Process

Culture
- People
- Process

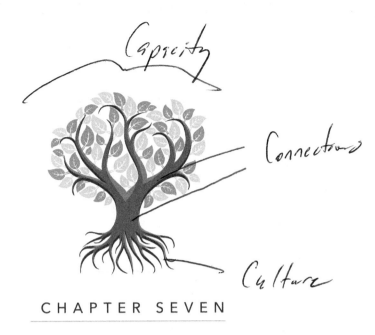

Capacity

Connections

Culture

CHAPTER SEVEN

Bringing It All Together

Our exploration of the model of your board is now complete. Likening the model to an oak tree, you know the three board dimensions of the canopy (capacity), the branches and trunk (connections), and the root system (culture). You have the knowledge and strategies to support your board to fulfill its potential—to become like the oak as it grows sturdier and more majestic.

This final chapter has four sections. The first is a summary of what we've covered. Next, I give you a few examples of how your board's three dimensions should be considered as you assess a board problem. Third, there's a reminder of the critical success factors of board development you want to keep in mind as you address the board problems you've assessed. Finally, I close with some personal thoughts.

In a Nutshell: What You Learned

We started this adventure with my invitation to you to reflect on this question: do you love your board? Do you remember your answer? While many boards may be great, many others fail to reach their potential to advance the missions the board members and executives are committed to and care about deeply. One reason for this is not focusing on the real cause of the board's weak functioning. Most executives and board members address *symptoms* of board problems and don't go deeper to discover and address *causes*.

We've explored together a model for understanding problems with your board at a much deeper level than is typical. You now understand the real causes of board problems, not just symptoms. You discovered every board issue or problem you've experienced, or will experience, fits within one of the three board dimensions: capacity, connection, and culture.

Now you have the insights to assess your board's issues in a new way and strategies for what to do about them. What's unique about the strategies is they're evidence-based—found effective through research—research based on the experiences of nonprofit executive directors like you. If you've been an executive director for a long time, you have new perspectives. If you're a newer executive director, you'll now avoid "barking up the wrong tree" when dealing with board issues.

Not all board problems fit neatly within capacity, connection, *or* culture. You probably already realize that, at times, you'll need to consider two or more of them as you and your board members work to identify the cause of the issue or problem you want to fix, In the next section, I give you some examples of how all three dimensions could come into play.

Capacity, Connection, or Culture? Consider All Three

In the Introduction, I shared that, through evidence-based practice, I discovered every problem, issue, or opportunity executive directors encounter with their boards falls into at least one of the three dimensions: capacity, connection, and culture. And each of those has both a people and a process aspect.

Some board problems will fit into all three. Let's review one example so you can see how this can play out. Remember James, executive director of Unleash Capabilities? Their fundraising challenges, discussed in Chapter Six, revealed both people—and process—capacity dimension issues. They not only didn't have the fundraising leaders they needed on the board, they didn't have a strong new board member recruitment process to get them. James' frustrations with his board and their lack of follow-up on fundraising commitments all contributed to a strained relationship—the board's connection dimension. And the beliefs and assumptions James' board members had about recruiting board members who could help with fundraising revealed they had issues within their board culture.

Your goal is to have an accurate and complete assessment of any board issue you're experiencing. Think of the entire tree: the canopy of leaves (capacity), the branches and trunk (connection), and the root system (culture). These are most often interdependent. So, consider all three board dimensions before concluding an assessment and deciding what to do.

The following examples show you how, using questions, you can approach assessing a board issue with all three dimensions in mind.

Issues with Board Recruitment

A capacity issue with board recruitment is commonly about the characteristics you need on the board. Is your strategic plan driving your board composition goals? What is it about our board composition you want to change to address an issue? What is your vision for it?

The connection dimension of your board comes into play here too. Are you engaging new board members early? Do you have an agreement as a team about the expectations of board members? As the executive director, is your perspective and involvement included in the process, reflecting a trusting board/executive relationship? Are there obstacles at the connection dimension causing problems with your board recruitment success?

Problems with recruitment can be about "fit"—how does a prospect "feel" to you all—an example of how the board's culture dimension creates recruitment challenges. What are the beliefs, assumptions, mindsets of the prospect? Are there different worldviews the prospect will bring, enriching the board's culture? Does your board value those worldviews?

Does your board value diversity, equity, and inclusion in ways that make your board recruitment system effective in creating the diverse board you desire?

Issues with Board Member Orientation

A problem with board member orientation may be a capacity process issue. Does your board have a consistent board member orientation? Does it cover both governance roles and responsibilities as well as information about your nonprofit? Is it clear who will do what, when? Do you find you're reinventing this every time new board members are elected?

There may be a connection issue with your board member orientation too. Are you building the relationships between the new board member and the rest of the board members? How are you launching *your* relationship with the new board member? What experiences are built into the "onboarding" process to focus on the relationship side of bringing this prospect onto the board?

Is board culture underlying the issue? How is the new board member being acculturated to your board? How are stories symbolizing board values being shared? Is there a board buddy who is "in the know" who can fill the new member in on how things are done and the meaning behind some of the ways the board operates?

And a final example . . .

Issues with the Board Chair/Executive Director Relationship

Challenges you experience in your relationship with the board chair are likely not only due to connection causes. Considering the capacity dimension, how much time are you and the board chair devoting to your relationship versus just working on your nonprofit's work? How much time does the board chair devote to meeting with you, and how often?

What about the connection dimension? <u>Have you communicated your expectations of each other clearly?</u> <u>Have you established agreements about how you'll work together?</u> <u>Does trust need to be strengthened?</u> <u>What do you have in common? Are you building identification-based trust?</u>

The culture dimension can come into play as well. Are there cultural differences in your backgrounds you need to be aware of and acknowledge? Is for-profit experience versus nonprofit experience influencing how you each look at things? How about gender differences? What about mindsets? Is a board member's glass half-full or half-empty?

To aim at the right target of change, nonprofit leaders sometimes need to go deeper and discover underlying causes. To be effective, you need to consider all three dimensions of your board and their people and process aspects. <u>Are the issues your board is struggling with being assessed or defined wholly and accurately?</u> Or are you and board <u>members trying to change things by addressing symptoms?</u>

This book is a resource for you. Use it to discover what's *really* going on with your board. You may identify aspects of the problem spanning all three of your board's dimensions when you do. If all three dimensions relate to a board problem you're tackling, you don't have to address all of them at once. But the value to you of realizing it's not just a capacity issue, for example, is you and your board members can prioritize action steps you know work. As a result, you'll be more effective and efficient in developing your board.

Assess, Then Develop the Board

Effective board development begins with assessing the need for change correctly. As a result of reading this book, you have new insights. Trust them. And trust yourself, working closely with your board members, to choose what to do first and then next. As with assessing the problem, when you're selecting what to do, consider strategies covered in all three dimensions. Make sure you aren't leaving something critical out of your assessment or leaving out an effective strategy.

Assess and agree upon what needs to improve or change. Then, together implement an effective board development process to achieve it. You've learned many useful strategies for addressing a variety of board problems executive directors experience. Remember what we covered in Chapter One? In addition to strategies, you learned the critical success factors of any board improvement effort: a nudge (maybe from you), the board chair, and intention. Effective board development may be triggered by a nudge but certainly requires an assessment correctly defining the issue; it then proceeds with intention and board chair leadership.

Effective board development is not a linear process. It's not dependent on the characteristics of your nonprofit or its life-cycle stage. For some nonprofits, board development is urgent and transformational; for others, it's an ongoing evolution. Just like any developmental process, boards committed to making an impact are never done. You know your board matters, and working to improve board effectiveness takes time and focus, but it's worth it. With this book in hand, your efforts will be more efficient and effective.

Love Your Board!

When nonprofit boards thrive, the executives working with them do too. What's at stake for executive directors who don't invest in their boards is the positive impact an effective board can have and maybe even their nonprofit's mission. What's at stake for you personally as the executive is the quality of your own daily experience of your board members—the benefits of thought leadership, leveraging relationships, and so much more. Effective board development results in a board, *your board*, getting the basics right, building a board infrastructure, becoming a strategic asset, attracting resources and social capital, engaging with the community in powerful ways, and supporting your success.

All aspects of board functioning can improve—meetings, board ownership, committee functioning, governance policies and practices, clarity of roles, leadership, team building, diversity, inclusion, and fundraising. Apply what you've learned here, and you'll gain a strong functioning board advancing the mission, leveraging and enhancing all you do.

I believe nonprofit executive directors are amazing people and can be outstanding leaders. I believe board members really care about the missions of the nonprofits they serve. They are driven by the desire to make a positive difference.

As an executive director, you are giving of yourself in many unique and wonderful ways. You are a nonprofit leader. And now, after completing this book, I hope you are an *inspired* nonprofit leader.

You have the insights and strategies you need to focus on the right issue and be the catalyst and facilitator of meaningful change for your board. Confidently step into your change-agent role—valuing and believing in your board as a strategic asset.

All this matters, plain and simple, because *you* matter and your board members matter.

Love your board! Nurture and invest in its members, and you'll be excited about the powerful impact you are making together.

Index

Made in United States
Orlando, FL
05 March 2023

30721119R10124